Developing Children as Researchers

Encouraging young children to create and carry out their own social research projects can have significant social and educational benefits. In addition, their research may help them to influence local and national policies and practices on issues that matter to them. To support this, *Developing Children as Researchers* acts as a practical guide to give teachers – and other adults who work with children – a set of structured, easy-to-follow session plans that will help children to become researchers in their own right.

Comprising ten session plans that have already been tried and tested in schools, this guide will assist you in supporting child researchers while helping you to develop the techniques for teaching research skills effectively. The session plans also ensure that children's views are heard and reflected by encouraging their active curiosity and investigation of issues that they may be concerned about. Forming a step-by-step guide, the ten sessions cover themes such as:

- starting the research process and identifying a research topic;
- the three key principles of research: be sceptical, systematic and ethical;
- choosing research participants and drawing up a research plan;
- the range of data collection and analysis methods;
- reporting the results of, and reflecting upon, a research project.

Children's research has often depended upon the support of academic researchers to provide resources and training. By making the research training and facilitation process more widely accessible, this guide will help remove the psychological and practical hurdles that teachers and others who regularly work with children might feel about helping children's research themselves.

Chae-Young Kim is an associate researcher at the Children's Research Centre, the Open University, UK. She has previously worked for UNICEF in South Korea.

Kieron Sheehy researches inclusive education and innovation pedagogies. He is an active member of the Open University's Children's Research Centre.

Lucinda Kerawalla is a former director of the Open University's Children's Research Centre. She also researches the technological support of classroom dialogues a

Developing Children as Researchers

A Practical Guide to Help Children Conduct Social Research

Chae-Young Kim, Kieron Sheehy
and Lucinda Kerawalla

Routledge
Taylor & Francis Group

LONDON AND NEW YORK

First published 2017
by Routledge
2 Park Square, Milton Park, Abingdon, Oxon OX14 4RN

and by Routledge
711 Third Avenue, New York, NY 10017

Routledge is an imprint of the Taylor & Francis Group, an informa business

British Library Cataloguing in Publication Data
A catalogue record for this book is available from the British Library

Library of Congress Cataloging in Publication Data
Names: Kim, Chae-Young, author. | Sheehy, Kieron, author. | Kerawalla, Cindy, author.
Title: Developing children as researchers : a practical guide to help children conduct social research / Chae-Young Kim, Kieron Sheehy and Cindy Kerawalla.
Description: Abingdon, Oxon ; New York, NY : Routledge, 2017. | Includes index.
Identifiers: LCCN 2016044658 | ISBN 9781138669253 (hardback) | ISBN 9781138669260 (pbk.) | ISBN 9781315618203 (ebook)
Subjects: LCSH: Social sciences--Study and teaching (Elementary) | Social sciences--Research--Study and teaching (Elementary) | Social sciences--Methodolgy--Study and teaching (Elementary)
Classification: LCC LB1584 .K54 2017 | DDC 300.71--dc23
LC record available at https://lccn.loc.gov/2016044658

ISBN: 978-1-138-66925-3 (hbk)
ISBN: 978-1-138-66926-0 (pbk)
ISBN: 978-1-315-61820-3 (ebk)

Typeset in Palatino
by Saxon Graphics Ltd, Derby

Printed and bound in Great Britain by
TJ International Ltd, Padstow, Cornwall

Contents

Acknowledgements

The authors would like to thank the staff, children and parents of Wavendon Gate School in Milton Keynes, UK, for working with them to help develop the first drafts of the session plans included in this book. They are also grateful to their colleagues at the Children's Research Centre at the Open University for using the session plans and giving useful feedback to improve them.

Of the authors, Chae-Young Kim would like to express her special gratitude to her husband Andrew for making creative suggestions whenever she felt stuck and for his untiring encouragement concerning her research about and with children. While compiling this book, she was also reminded of her father, Mahn-Gon Kim, an educator in South Korea, who has stressed the significance of developing children's independent thinking skills and creativity in learning.

Finally the authors thank Emily Harper-Barlow for drawing illustrations which have made the text much more lively and accessible.

Introduction

Would you like to help children to be researchers in their own right? If so, this book is for you. It contains ten ready-made session plans that you can use to help children to carry out their own social research projects. If you have not done social research yourself, or if your research skills are a little rusty, you may be worried that this may be a barrier to you supporting child researchers. However, the session plans in this book are designed for someone like you and, by using the plans with children, you can also learn about or enhance your own understanding of social research.

You may be wondering why working with child researchers is a good thing to do. Some people are interested in supporting child researchers to ensure that their views are heard and better reflected in the production of evidence about them. Other people wish children's opinions to be taken into account during the decision-making processes that affect their lives. Also, it has been suggested that the practice of children conducting their own research has educational benefits such as raised self-esteem and confidence, and improvements in literacy, numeracy, communication, information processing, critical thinking and higher-order thinking skills. As a result, children have been helped to conduct their own research in a wide range of settings such as schools and local communities.

The following quotes are from primary school teachers who have worked with child researchers and illustrate the value of this work:

> Most of us, most of time, we probably underestimate hugely what children can do. Through this initiative, they learn a range of skills to apply to a topic of their own choice, investigate and present it in a rigorous way.

It is possible to find out about something that they are really interested in and, if it is well-researched, it can have an impact.

In the past, children have usually relied upon the assistance of academic researchers to support them in carrying out their research projects. However, what about non-academics who are interested in working with young researchers? While some books are available on how non-academics can facilitate children's research projects, they do not contain ready-made session plans that can be used straight away with children. Such books often assume a certain level of expertise, or additional work is needed in order to develop their content into something practical before they can actually be used. This may be unappealing to those who might wish to 'try out' facilitating children's research but who may not regard themselves as sufficiently familiar with social research to teach children research skills or who do not have additional time to devote to developing their own resources. This book has been written to help remove such psychological and practical hurdles by presenting readily implementable research support session plans. The plans should be accessible to any adults who work with children who might be interested in investigating social issues systematically, critically and ethically.

Before using the session plans, it may be useful to know some background about how children have become more actively involved in research over the years, and the social and educational benefits this may offer.

Children as active social agents and authors of knowledge

Views about what makes a good childhood and which activities are suitable for children have changed throughout history. For example, the idea that a child's main activity is school education was not always shared widely. In countries with universal (or near-universal) primary and even secondary education, particularly before national education systems were established, many children were involved in economic activities and worked alongside adults in fields, family-run businesses or factories. In these countries, children's participation in school-based education increased gradually over time due to a combination of factors including technological advances in workplaces, improvements in the conditions of adult labour markets and the availability of decent school education (Basu, 1999). Even in current times, ideas about what children should be doing with their time can vary across different societies and cultures.

Also, the way in which academic researchers view the role of children in relation to research has varied and changed considerably in recent years. Until about two decades ago, children were seen mainly as the objects of investigation and most researchers saw them only as sources to collect data about and from (Green and Hill, 2005). This started to change as more researchers increasingly began to see them as 'subjects' who could exercise their own agency[1] in research. This meant that they began to involve children in more active roles than just as passive sources of data. Therefore, children became involved in different stages of the research process alongside adult researchers: for example, as co-researchers, taking part in designing the project, collecting and analysing data, and disseminating the findings. Furthermore, the idea of enabling children to become primary investigators also emerged as part of this wider shift in reconceptualising the role of children in research.

A significant driver behind the change in the role of children in research was the adoption of the UN Convention on the Rights of the Child (UNCRC) in 1989. The UNCRC articulated children's rights to participate in matters that affect them and their lives. This legally binding international document has been a major rationale for an increasing number of researchers to explore children's active role in research and engagement in public activities in society more widely. Children are increasingly seen as active 'social agents' who contribute to the construction of the social worlds around them in the present rather than as mainly passive objects to socialise into adulthood. This perspective has led to initiatives in which children are actively involved in the production of research evidence about their lives and experiences, informing the policies and practices that concern them.

However, there is a difference between children being co-researchers alongside adults and being the primary investigators. When children are involved in research alongside adult researchers, there is often a risk that these adults make the main decisions in the process. In these cases, children work on 'adult-led' agendas and/or under 'adult-designed' research frameworks. In comparison, where children conduct research as its primary investigators, it is they who make such decisions throughout the process from the identification of the research topic to those regarding the dissemination of the findings. In this situation, the children are facilitated to take on full ownership of, and responsibility for, their research.

Children have been helped to carry out their own research in diverse settings but most frequently in their schools (see, for example, Bucknall, 2009, 2012; Kellett *et al.*, 2004; Roberts and Nash, 2009). The topics the children choose to research can vary: for example, some choose to investigate school practices (e.g. school uniforms, the difficulty of maths teaching, classroom behaviour management, extracurricular classes) and others conduct research about people's relationships in the school (e.g. children's relationships with teachers, the experiences of children who are smaller than their peers), while yet others choose to explore what children think about issues beyond the school (e.g. the nature of parents' jobs and its impact on their relationships with their children, children's worries, the social nature of children's TV viewing, children's views about going to university, children's views about keeping animals captive in zoos). The findings from children's research in school settings are shared and discussed with their teachers, parents and other children, and some of them are applied to improve relevant practices.

Children may also have opportunities to conduct research outside school. For example, Kellett (2011) describes how 11-year-old child researchers conducted research for the UK Department of Transport on children's mobility by researching topics which included travelling to school, the experience of child wheelchair users and children's views about safety at bus stops. There have also been similar projects in India, South Africa and Ghana where children conducted research on their mobility and access to local public services (Lolichen *et al.*, 2006). Children in special circumstances such as those in care have been supported to conduct research too. This helped to build a better understanding of the services they are offered as well as raising their self-esteem and confidence (Michail and Kellett, 2015).

The educational benefits of children's research

Through conducting research on issues that interest them and then, with the knowledge produced, taking part in decision-making processes concerning those issues, children can learn how to address social questions constructively and to participate in democratic decision-making processes more meaningfully. This means that by being active social agents in the present, they can also learn to become more effective citizens in the future. Other benefits that children are reported to gain through doing research include, as mentioned earlier, raised confidence and self-esteem (e.g. Kellett, 2010, 2011; Kellett *et al.*, 2004; Lolichen *et al.*, 2006; Roberts and Nash, 2009). As a result of learning research skills and by carrying out a project themselves, children realise what they are capable of and understand how they might better approach future challenges. In addition, some researchers suggest that children gain cognitive benefits through learning about research and from applying their skills to investigating an actual topic. These benefits include improved literacy and numeracy skills, information processing and higher-order thinking skills (e.g. Bucknall, 2012; Kellett, 2005). Indeed, the primary school children who took part in the testing of the session plans in this book also highlighted the learning benefits of their experiences. In particular, they mentioned learning to think critically about what they used to take for granted, learning to think about the underlying causes of social phenomena and to be more reflective about their own biases about particular issues. For example, they said:

> We do not take things as they are and we question why things are the way they are.
>
> (Child researcher, age 11)

> I learned that you've got to be critical and that you can be too biased.
>
> (Child researcher, age 8)

Teachers and other adults who are interested in children's research often believe in child-centred approaches to education. Some of the potential educational benefits from children's research may be identified by comparing it with a child-centred approach, in particular, a form of inquiry-based learning. Figure 0.1 shows a conceptual framework of four different forms of inquiry-based learning. All four forms involve children engaging with either closed or open-ended questions to find answers to them instead of passively receiving prescribed knowledge from their teachers. Of these

Information active: children explore a knowledge base by searching for existing answers to their own closed questions	**Discovery active**: children investigate their own open-ended questions in interaction with the knowledge base of the subject area
Information responsive: children explore the knowledge base of the subject area in response to closed questions framed by a teacher	**Discovery responsive**: children pursue open-ended questions framed by a teacher in interaction with the knowledge base of the subject area

Figure 0.1 Types of inquiry-based learning: a conceptual framework
Source: Adapted from Healy and Jenkins, 2009: 26.

four forms, the 'discovery active' type is most similar to conducting research as it involves children investigating an open-ended question that they identify themselves in interaction with an existing knowledge base around the topic.

The main purpose of conducting research is to produce knowledge that will advance our understanding of certain issues and/or inform relevant practices and policies, whereas the aim of inquiry-based learning as a pedagogy is to achieve particular learning outcomes. As a result of conducting their own research, children may gain some 'educational' benefits, while, as a result of participating in the 'discovery active' type of inquiry-based learning, they might also produce some original findings that are significant in the subject area. However, these outcomes are not always those that are intended or expected from the respective activities and they are *additional* to the core purposes of each. This suggests that while there are certainly overlaps between the two activities, there is also a conceptual distinction between children conducting research and the discovery active form of inquiry-based learning (Kim, 2016).

Some people suggest that child-centred education such as the 'discovery active' type of inquiry-based learning can help children to learn better by having more control over their own learning and prepare them better for their future lives where the nature of knowledge and skills required for employment continue to change (see Schweisfurth, 2013). In addition, it is believed that a range of children's rights can be best upheld in the context of child-centred education. Upon this rationale, both the United Nations Educational, Scientific and Cultural Organization (UNESCO) and the United Nations Children's Fund (UNICEF), the UN agencies concerned with children's education and development, endorse child-centred education (Schweisfurth, 2013). Ultimately this is where children's research can be a way to ensure their rights to participate in matters and decision-making processes that concern them and also be a pedagogical tool for their educational benefits without compromising either. This means that if children's research is carried out in the context of child-centred education where both children's participation rights and their rights to education are supported equally, it is unlikely to slip into the common trap of being regarded as a tool for 'practising' research simply for its potential educational benefits. In such contexts, children's research will also be respected as being worthwhile in its own right and the children's findings will be taken into account more seriously.

▉ Adult 'facilitation' and adult 'management' of children's research

A big issue when helping children to conduct their own research concerns the type of support offered by adults. Although children are able to exercise their agency throughout the research process, in most cases and to varying degrees, they require support from adults at various points in their projects. Adult research students, such as those studying for a doctorate, usually require supervision throughout their projects. Also academic researchers often collaborate with one another to enhance their pool of expertise. So, children's need of adult support does not suggest that they are unable to lead their own projects. However, adults need to be careful that their involvement maintains the right balance of simply facilitating the progress of the children's research – thus enabling them to continue to lead it – as opposed to managing it or taking it over (Kellett, 2011). Table 0.1 compares some examples of adult involvement with children's research where it may be seen to be facilitating or managing it.

All the session plans in this book have been designed based on the principle of adults facilitating children's research rather than managing it. The next chapter briefly discusses some practical suggestions for using the session plans in the book.

Table 0.1 Examples of adult facilitation vs adult management of children's research

Facilitation	*Management*
Enabling: supporting the idea that children can undertake their own research	Judging: suggesting that a child's idea is not worthy enough to research
Supporting: paving the way for children with gatekeepers (e.g. in accessing their research participants)	Controlling: controlling access to research participants
Helping: helping children with some of the legwork rather than the design work (e.g. transcribing interviews, number crunching)	Influencing: allowing adult interest or agendas to influence what children investigate
Empowering: actively seeking dissemination platforms for child researchers	Manipulating: using the findings of children's research to suit adult agendas

Source: Adapted from Kellett, 2011.

References

Basu, K. (1999) 'Child labour: Cause, consequence and cure with remarks on international labour standards', *Journal of Economic Literature*, 37(3): 1083–1119.

Bucknall, S. (2009) *Children as Researchers: Exploring Issues and Barriers in English Primary Schools*. PhD thesis. The Open University.

Bucknall, S. (2012) *Children as Researchers in Primary Schools: Choice, Voice and Participation*. London and New York: Routledge.

Green, S. and Hill, M. (2005) 'Researching children's experience: Methods and methodological issues.' In S. Greene and Hogan, D. (eds) *Researching Children's Experience: Approaches and Methods*. London: Sage.

Healy, M. and Jenkins, A. (2009) *Developing Undergraduate Research and Inquiry*. York: The Higher Education Academy.

Kellett, M. (2005) *How to Develop Children as Researchers: A Step by Step Guide to Teaching the Research Process*. London: Paul Chapman Publishing.

Kellett, M. (2010) 'WeCan2: Exploring the implications of young people with learning disabilities engaging in their own research', *European Journal of Special Needs Education*, 25(1): 31–44.

Kellett, M. (2011) 'Empowering children and young people as researchers: Overcoming barriers and building capacity', *Child Indicator Research*, 4: 205–219.

Kellett, M., Forrest, R., Dent, N. and Ward, S. (2004) '"Just teach us the skills please, we'll do the rest": Empowering 10-year-olds as active researchers', *Children & Society*, 18: 329–343.

Kim, C.-Y. (2016) 'Participation or pedagogy?: Ambiguities and tensions surrounding the facilitation of children as researchers', *Childhood*. Ahead of print. DOI: 10.1177/0907568216643146

Lolichen, P.J., Shenoy, J., Shetty, A., Nash, C. and Venkatesh, M. (2006) 'Children in the driver's seat', *Children's Geographies*, 4(3): 347–357.

Michail, S. and Kellett, M. (2015) 'Child-led research in the context of Australian social welfare practice', *Child and Family Social Work*, 20(4): 387–395.

Roberts, A. and Nash, J. (2009) 'Enabling students to participate in school improvement through a student as researchers programme', *Improving Schools*, 12: 184–187.

Schweisfurth, M. (2013) *Learner-centred Education in International Perspective: Whose Pedagogy for Whose Development?* London: Routledge.

Note

1 There is not a universally accepted definition of agency. However, agency is often conceptualised as human capacity to think and act independently.

Suggestions for using the session plans

Inclusive and exploratory practice

We hope that the session plans in this book are self-explanatory and easy to use without requiring much preparation beforehand. They have been designed for adults with little or no social research training. As you implement the plans with children, you will also increase your own understanding of the research process. Alternatively, if you have some prior research experience, we hope the session plans become convenient ready-made resources and save you the time of developing your own from scratch.

While each session plan contains all the explanations you may need, we thought some general practical suggestions might be useful for you in advance of actually using them. These suggestions are based on a two-year pilot study of testing the session plans, the experiences of colleagues who also used them and evidence from existing research studies on facilitating children's research.

Working with children of mixed abilities

The session plans have been designed mainly for use by adults who work with primary-school-age children and were developed through working with academically mixed (in terms of reading, writing and maths skills) groups of children who were 8–11 years of age. We tested the plans with mixed-ability groups because children's research projects have been criticised for often selecting those who are deemed 'academically able'. At the end of the projects the children's level of understanding of research concepts and methods and the quality of their research outputs varied. It was interesting that while these variances seemed to be related to their assessed academic abilities, the quality of their research did not depend entirely on them. Not surprisingly, good reading, writing and numeracy skills can help children to do well in designing data collection tools, analysing data and creating materials to present their research findings. However, children's enthusiasm about their research topic, their diligence and perseverance throughout the process and how creatively they made use of their own skills when dealing with various tasks also mattered. The idea that children of all abilities should be offered a chance to conduct research is important. For example, children with learning difficulties, with appropriate support, successfully conducted a research project that changed the way they took part in local council youth service meetings (Kellett, 2010).

Although the session plans were developed with upper-primary-level children, they can also be used with older or younger children. This is because the main purpose of the plans is not to impart some fixed pieces of knowledge but to facilitate children to acquire an approach to explore issues of their own interest and choice. The session plans do this by helping them to learn some core research concepts and skills and then supporting them to carry out their own research projects. The level and quality of children's thinking and discussion during this process are determined mainly by the children themselves, and partly by their adult facilitator, but not by the session plans alone.

Thinking, discussing and exploring towards an understanding

The session plans involve two main tasks for children to undertake:

- to learn how to conduct social research; and
- actually to carry out a research project.

The session plans have been designed with a particular pedagogic approach in mind. As each new concept is introduced, children are asked to think about and explore actively what it might mean. Then, by talking about what they think and by drawing upon their adult facilitator's guidance during this exploratory thinking, they adjust their initial ideas about the concept to a more accurate understanding of it. When children's initial answers to the adult's questions are not appropriate, instead of 'correcting' them immediately, the adult can ask them to think further about the question or ask some further questions to help them to get closer to the concept.

If you have not had any or much social research training, you might feel somewhat uncertain about leading the process described above. However, based on our experiences, a reading of the session plans beforehand and having them physically present during the sessions for reference purposes should prepare you sufficiently for your role. It is also a good strategy to be open with children from the start that the sessions will be an exploratory learning process for all the participants including yourself. Some people might not feel comfortable about this approach, but often children appreciate the fact that their teachers or adults may not know answers to everything and they enjoy doing something that may be challenging for their teachers and other adults as well as for themselves.

Exploring solutions to questions and dilemmas in the research process

There may be times when you are unable to support the children with satisfactory solutions or approaches to certain questions or dilemmas which can arise in research. In these instances, you could suggest exploring the issues with the children in a future session. Towards the end of this book, we have suggested a list of some further reading on social research methods which you could use as a starting point for such exploration. However, these ambiguous moments should not discourage children from continuing their research journey. Even very experienced researchers will find themselves in situations where they are unable to think of any clear solutions. Exploring how to solve ambiguous questions and dilemmas is part of learning about and carrying out research. As you will see in the session plans, any issues that cannot be resolved need to be reported as part of the limitations of the research project and it is useful to discuss with the children, and later with the audience of the project, how they may have influenced the research findings.

Building the practice of working together

If you work with a group of children in using the session plans, the relationship between the children is a particularly important part of the research process. It will be helpful to discuss with them early on in the process that they respect each other's ideas at all times and help each other if this is needed. During the sessions, it is important for children to feel comfortable about speaking about what they think because this is an important part of how they develop their understanding of research concepts and skills. In order for them to do this, there should be a sense of respect and an understanding that everyone (including the adult) can speak about different ideas with each other. The first session plan therefore suggests deciding on and agreeing the 'ground rules' of working together in all the research sessions.

Learning about and doing research simultaneously

The session plans have been designed so that as children learn about each stage of the research process, they simultaneously develop their own research projects. This is mainly because our experience suggests that children are often keen to start their projects before the completion of their research training. However, you can be flexible about this and, depending on the characteristics of the children, you might decide to complete the research training first before helping them to conduct their research projects.

Working towards flexible application of the session plans

By designing session plans that can be used straight away, we hoped to reduce the psychological and practical hurdles that readers might experience if they had to develop their own series of session plans to support children's research. However, we do not expect the session plans to be followed mechanically word by word. In particular, once you have become familiar with the research process and how to use the session plans, you may decide to modify them to better suit your own teaching style and the characteristics of the children you are working with.

Facilitating children's research inside and outside school

While many research examples in the session plans are set in a school context, we hope this does not give the impression that the session plans can be used only in a school context. For example, children's services workers or parents can easily use them in non-school contexts. Children who have learned the key principles and skills of social research based on the examples in the session plans might decide to do a project on a topic that is set outside school. As long as it is manageable by themselves, children's research projects do not have to be about school-related issues. Alternatively, if you are working with children outside school, you can modify some of the examples in the sessions to suit your own context.

When children need individual support

During the research process there will be stages when children require more individual support. These typically include: when they are formulating their initial ideas into a research topic that satisfies the criteria for a social research project they can manage themselves; when they are designing their data collection tools; and when they start to analyse their data. At these times, in addition to supporting them individually, it can be helpful to get them to review each other's ideas and work in progress. Peer review of research proposals, work in progress and final outputs is a common practice in a research community. We have found that children respond well to giving each other feedback, and can be constructively critical and informatively helpful about each other's work. These peer-reviewing opportunities also allow children to check and modify their own understanding of research concepts and skills.

Some children will progress faster with their projects than others. In these cases, it is often useful if the faster children support those who are slower. This may be a good opportunity for the helping child to reflect on their own project by being involved in another one and allows them to remain actively involved in the class rather than waiting for others to 'catch up with them'.

When children require more individual support, and especially if one adult is working with a large number of children, the adult might feel too stretched to help out everyone simultaneously. We have found that if the number of children in the group is more than ten, it can be helpful for more than one adult to act as the children's research facilitators.

Timetabling the research sessions

Each session is expected to last approximately one hour and 15 minutes. However, the sessions can be shorter or longer than this, depending on how much time is set aside for children's thinking and discussions. If they are longer than an hour, children may need a short break during the session. Depending on the availability of time, each session can also be divided into two or more shorter sessions or run in a way that suits your circumstances.

When we tested the session plans, we ran them once a week after the school's curricular hours. Between some sessions, longer intervals may be needed to allow children sufficient time to make progress with their own projects – in particular, time to design their data collection tools, to collect and analyse data, and to produce materials with which to report findings. The timetable used in our pilot study may give some ideas about how to schedule the sessions over the entire process (see Table 0.2). In our timetable, for example, two weeks were allocated to let children design their data collection tools. However, if children have more time to work on this outside the research sessions, less time could be allocated. We have found that it is always helpful to factor some flexibility into the timetabling.

Table 0.2 A sample timetable of weekly research sessions

Week	Content
1	Session 1. What is social research?
2	Session 2. Starting the research process: identifying a research topic
3	Session 3. Three key principles: be sceptical, be systematic and be ethical
4	Session 4. Data collection method one: questionnaires
5	Session 5. Data collection method two: interviews
6	Session 6. Further data collection methods: observations and using visual materials
7	Session 7. Choosing research participants and drawing up a research plan
8–9	Children design their data collection tools.
10–11	Data collection period. Children could drop in or arrange one-to-one appointments if they require any assistance with their data collection.
12	Session 8. Analysing data by counting up
13	Session 9. Analysing data by noticing meanings
14–15	Children analyse their data.
16	Session 10. Reporting and reflecting on social research
17–18	Children complete their research presentation materials. They could drop in or arrange one-to-one appointments if they need assistance.
19	Presentation practice
20	Presentation of the research projects at an assembly

Setting your own benchmarks for children's research outputs

This book introduces the process, principles and skills to conduct social research rigorously, as well as some practical templates to refer to, but it does not intend to prescribe what the final outputs of children's research should look like. We have found that the quality of children's outputs varies considerably, with some resembling what academic researchers might produce and others less so. However, what is important is whether the research that is produced is meaningful for the children, so we hope that you and the children will set your own benchmarks to achieve rather than simply reproducing something similar to what has been done elsewhere. While working with the social research framework in this book, we hope that children will get the most out of the social research process by applying it creatively and producing outcomes that bear their own imprint.

Finding resources required for the sessions

Given that the amount and variety of available resources may vary in the contexts where you may choose to use the session plans, we have designed them in such a way that it should be possible to use them with only a few resources. Most sessions can be implemented by using only the activity and information sheets and other photocopiable resources that are attached to them. The resources are inserted just after the relevant session plans. Teachers with whom we worked found this format allowed them quickly to relate the activities described in the sessions to the required activity and information sheets. Possible answers and discussion points for these resources are inserted within the session plans in order to help you to keep track of the flow of the sessions. While our aim was to make the session plans implementable with few resources, you may decide to use different physical and information technology resources to personalise the sessions to suit the needs and interests of your child researchers.

What is social research?

Session objectives

- Start to develop an understanding of what social research is
- Understand the kinds of evidence that are used in social research
- Start to develop an understanding of the research process

Key vocabulary

Social research, research topic, research question, evidence, data, analyse (analysis)

Resources

- Copies of Activity Sheet 1.1, and Information Sheets 1.1 and 1.2
- A large sheet of paper
- A whiteboard or some sticky notes
- Folders in which the children can store their activity and information sheets throughout their research process

Warm-up activity: who is in our group?

 If the children in the group are new to one another, this activity is suggested to give them an opportunity to get to know each other. Otherwise, proceed to the next activity.

Group the children into pairs and, for a few minutes, ask them to find out the following information about each other: their names, what they like, what they dislike, what they are good at, what they might be expecting from the research sessions and so on. Then, each pair introduce their partners to the other children in turn.

Deciding the ground rules: how will we work together?

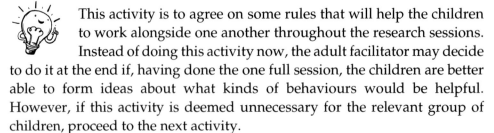 This activity is to agree on some rules that will help the children to work alongside one another throughout the research sessions. Instead of doing this activity now, the adult facilitator may decide to do it at the end if, having done the one full session, the children are better able to form ideas about what kinds of behaviours would be helpful. However, if this activity is deemed unnecessary for the relevant group of children, proceed to the next activity.

1. Suggest that they decide on some rules that everybody in the group should observe throughout the sessions. Then ask what they would like to include in these rules and write down their suggestions on sticky notes or the whiteboard (see some examples in Box 1.1).

   The adult facilitator may also make some suggestions. When there are too many suggestions, choose the most important rules by majority voting.

Box 1.1 The ground rules might include:

- Listen carefully when other people speak
- Respect other people's ideas
- Give reasons when speaking about an idea
- Give reasons when disagreeing with an idea
- Help each other out when needed

---

2. Put the chosen rules on a large sheet of paper and display it on one side of the room throughout the remaining sessions. When needed, draw the children's attention to these ground rules.

What is research?

1. Ask the children what they think 'research' is. Put examples of their thoughts on sticky notes and display them on a board or write them down on the whiteboard.

 Some children may say that research is looking in books or on the Internet to find information or an answer to a question. Strictly speaking, simply locating what other people have made available is not research. However, the adult facilitator may decide to let the children call such activity 'everyday research' to differentiate it from 'research'.

2. When the children have run out of answers, explain the definition in Box 1.2. Then discuss with the children how this definition is different from what they initially thought research was.

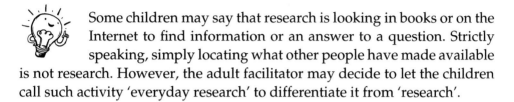

Box 1.2 Research is a process by which a person:

Finds facts about a topic that no one knows much about, or (an) answer(s) to a question that no one yet knows; or (when the existing facts or answers are not convincing), investigates them anew to see whether different facts or answers can be found.

A 'process' involves a series of stages of activities to complete a task.

3. Help the children to build an understanding of what research is by asking them the following three questions and discussing their responses.

 In discussing these questions, the children may give examples of natural science research instead of social research. The subsequent activities will help them to understand the differences between them.

*   Can you find all the information that you would like to know in books or on the Internet?
*   Can you think of a question that no one yet knows the answer to (something that you cannot find in a book or on the Internet)?

If the children struggle to think of any examples, suggest the following questions and ask what they think about them: 'what do children in my school think about school assembly?', 'do children in my neighbourhood want to go to university, and why or why not?' and 'are boys in my school more likely than girls to enjoy reading for fun?'

- Can you think of a topic or question about which some people have suggested answers but not all people agree on them?

    If the children struggle to think of any examples, suggest the examples in Box 1.3 and discuss what they think about them.

Box 1.3 Some issues of ongoing debates

Are rich people happier than those who are not rich?

Some research has found that the rich tend to be happier with their lives than those who are less well-off. However, there are continuing debates on the answer to this question.

Why do some children in poor countries go to work instead of going to school?

A number of studies have been carried out on this topic. While many of them suggest that the main reason is because their families are poor, others suggest that children of some poor families still go to school. Studies are still going on regarding possible causes of child labour and also its consequences in different local and country contexts.

A possible further discussion topic

Researchers sometimes raise questions over the findings of other researchers or about what we have commonly taken for granted. In many parts of the world, people once thought women were not able to think as rationally as men, so they were not given the right to vote or the right to own property, but now not many people think this is true. Research contributes to humankind's continuous exploration to find 'what may be true'.

Research looks for evidence: understanding evidence in social research in comparison to evidence in natural science research

1. Explain to the children that there are different types of research. What they will learn about and carry out themselves during these sessions is 'social research', which is different from 'natural science research'.

   Ask and discuss with the children how the two types of research might be different: 'social research' is research about the thoughts, feelings, behaviours and experiences of persons, while 'natural science research' is research about the physical world including physical objects, natural phenomena and the laws of nature.

2. Distribute copies of Activity Sheet 1.1. The children in small groups should discuss the questions on the activity sheet for a few minutes.

   In a plenary, each group presents what they discussed. Lead the plenary discussion based on Box 1.4.

Box 1.4 Possible answers to Activity Sheet 1.1

If the children are social researchers:

- *What might they be interested in investigating?*
  What do villagers want to do about the house? Are there any differences between what adults and what children want to do about the house?

  How does the house influence villagers' choices of travel routes around it? Are there any differences between those of adults and those of children? What makes these differences?

- *How would they investigate the questions?*
  They may ask the villagers, including both the adults and the children, what they want to do about the house, which route they choose to take when they need to pass by the house and the reasons for this. They then examine the answers.

If the children are natural science researchers:

- *What might they be interested in investigating?*
  Are there indeed unexplained phenomena that might be suspected to be caused ghosts in the house?

● *How would they investigate the question?*
They may put machines in the house to see whether they can detect any energy or air waves that might be a sign of ghostly movements, or they may use video cameras to see whether they can film any ghostly phenomena.

3. Ask and discuss with the children, based on Box 1.5, the similarities and differences between what social researchers and natural science researchers do to answer their questions.

Box 1.5 Research and 'evidence'

Both social researchers and natural science researchers try to find 'evidence' to answer their questions. When researchers tell other people about what they have found out, they also need to tell them what evidence they found to support it so that others can judge whether their evidence really supports the answer(s).

The kinds of things that social researchers and natural science researchers use as evidence are different. Social researchers usually collect evidence about people's thoughts, feelings and behaviours, whereas natural science researchers collect evidence to do with physical objects and natural phenomena.

The research process: imagining a research journey

1. Explain that learning about and doing social research may be compared to taking a well-organised foreign trip. Then discuss briefly with the children what they might do before, during and after a trip to a foreign country.

2. Distribute copies of Information Sheet 1.1. Use the information sheet to compare what doing research requires with what is required when taking a well-organised foreign trip. The children will not understand some research words or the three key principles in research ('be sceptical', 'be systematic' and 'be ethical'), so reassure them that they will learn about them in later sessions.

3. Distribute copies of Information Sheet 1.2, which shows the stages of the social research process. Go through the stages of the social research process with the children.

Where the children do not understand particular words, explain that they are almost like 'foreign words' with which they will become more familiar over time as they go through the research process. For preliminary understanding of some key research words, ask the children to think briefly about what 'research topic', 'research question', 'data' and 'analyse' might mean before explaining each term to them, as in Box 1.6.

 In addition to their initial research training, researchers usually continue to learn more about doing research throughout their research process and also when they move on to do another research project.

> ## Box 1.6 Definitions of some research words
>
> A 'research topic' is a subject or issue that the researcher decides to investigate by conducting research. In particular, if this is in the form of a question, it is called a 'research question'.
>
> 'Data' are all the information that the researcher collects to investigate their research topic or question. The researcher looks for 'evidence' in the data to address the research topic or question.
>
> 'Analyse' means to examine something closely and thoroughly. 'Analysis' is a noun form of 'analyse'. The researcher needs to analyse their data to find evidence that relates to their research topic or question.
>
> For example, a research topic might be 'TV viewing of the children in my class'. This research topic might be formed into the research question 'what do the children in my class watch on TV and why?' In this case, the researcher might ask questions concerning the research topic or question to the children in their class. All the answers from the children would be data, and then these data would be analysed to find evidence that addresses the research topic or question.

Wrap up

1. Discuss with the children any questions or comments that they might have from the session.

2. Ask them to start thinking about what topics or questions they might be interested in researching.

3. Distribute empty folders. Explain that they will keep all the activity and information sheets from these sessions in these folders, and that keeping the research folders will be useful to remind them of what they are learning and doing throughout their research process. For example, it will be useful when they write up their research to remember what they did at each stage of the process as they need to tell their audience about it.

If I am a researcher

Ghosts in the house

In my village there are rumours that ghosts appear in a house that has been empty for about ten years. These rumours mean that the villagers avoid walking near the house, especially at night.

If you are a social researcher, what would you be interested in investigating about this situation? Then how would you investigate it?

If you are a natural science researcher, what would you be interested in investigating about this situation? Then how would you investigate it?

INFORMATION SHEET 1.1

Taking a well-organised foreign trip and doing research

Taking a well-organised foreign trip	Doing research
• Think about what I am interested to see and experience and then decide on which country to visit	• Think about what I am interested to investigate and then decide on a topic or question
• Read about the country in advance to be able to appreciate what I will see and experience when I am there	• Search for background information about the topic or existing research findings to help me clarify what I want to investigate about it and to decide how I will go about investigating it
• Learn about how to behave abroad and the things I need to be aware of throughout the trip	• Learn the key principles to follow throughout the research process (i.e. be sceptical, be systematic and be ethical – we will learn about these in a subsequent session)
• Learn some useful foreign words • Learn new skills (e.g. first aid skills)	• Learn research words • Learn some new skills (i.e. those to help me to find evidence about my topic)
• Make an overall plan about what I will see, where I will sleep and what I will eat and so on over the number of days I will spend in the country (so I will maximise my experience of the country) • This plan may be adjusted during the trip depending on contingencies	• Make an overall plan on what I will do in order to investigate the chosen topic over the number of days available to do the research (in order to investigate the topic most appropriately) • This plan may be adjusted during the research process depending on contingencies
• During the trip, take pictures and write notes of my thoughts and feelings to keep a record (this will help me to remember the trip later on)	• Write a research diary about key events and thoughts throughout the research process and keep a research folder (this will help me when I need to write up my research)
• Reflect on how the trip was for me • Tell other people about what the trip was like	• Reflect upon the research experience • Tell other people about the research and its findings

The social research process

Identify what to investigate – a topic which can be in the form of a question

Make a plan about what to do in order to investigate the topic (for example, about whom to collect data from and/or about, how to collect and analyse the data, and with whom and how to share the findings)

Make (a) research tool(s) to use to collect the data

Collect data

Analyse data

Organise the findings from the analysis and **decide the conclusion(s) or answer(s)** in response to the topic or question

Share the findings with other people whom they may concern and **reflect** on the research experience

Starting the research process
Identifying a research topic

Session objectives

- Know how to identify a 'good' social research topic or question
- Start to identify a research topic or a research question
- Understand that finding background information about a potential research topic, or looking at some similar existing research, may be useful

Key vocabulary

- Research topic, research question

Resources

- Copies of Activity Sheets 2.1 and 2.2, and Information Sheet 2.1

Introduction

Review the key concepts from Session 1 by asking and discussing the following questions with the children: 'what is research?', 'what is social research about?', 'how is social research different from natural science research?' and 'what does the research process involve?'

What is a 'good' research topic like?

1. Check whether any of the children have thoughts about what they might like to investigate for their social research.

   Explain that a topic needs to meet some rules for it to be suitable for social research that 'they can manage'. Then distribute copies of 'My social research topic checklist' (Information Sheet 2.1). Read through the list with the children.

2. Distribute copies of Activity Sheet 2.1. The children check whether each of the topics and questions on the activity sheet is good for the social research that they might conduct, using the 'My social research topic checklist', and think about whether it is, why it is and if it is not, why it is not.

   In a plenary, the children present what they think about each topic or question on the activity sheet. Lead the discussion based on the information in Box 2.1.

Box 2.1 Suggested answers for Activity Sheet 2.1

Question 1: This question is too big for a child to be able to address because it has to target all primary school children across the country.

Question 2: This topic reflects the researcher's personal opinion about homework and assumes that homework may be boring to everyone and all the time. If the researcher asks someone, 'what do you think about boring homework?', it is likely to lead her or him to take it as a fact that homework is boring and to express their opinion based on that idea. Deleting 'boring' from the topic will make it a good research topic.

Question 3: This is a good question for social research that a child would be able to carry out.

Question 4: This is not a social research question as it is about a natural phenomenon. Furthermore, an answer to this question will be available in a book or on the Internet and it is very likely that no one disputes that answer. Hence it probably does not require researching.

Question 5: It is not certain why it is worth investigating this topic. In other words, what difference would it make knowing more about this topic?

Question 6: The process of researching this topic may involve showing a violent film which might cause distress to very young children, and their parents might not be happy about it either.

Identifying my social research topic

Distribute copies of Activity Sheet 2.2, 'Identifying my social research topic'. The children try to think of their research topic, using the activity sheet.

If any of the children wish to conduct research in a pair or in a group, they can do this activity together. However, it will be useful for all of them to keep activity sheets individually for the benefit of individual reference.

 Some children might already have thought of a research topic or research question. In this case, they can also do the activity to check or refine it. Other children may continue to change or adjust their research topic up until when they need to start making data collection tools. The children need to decide on their topics before Session 7 when they draw up their overall research plans. This is because after Session 7 they start to make their data collection tools and then collect data. The children's progress with identifying their topic will need to be checked regularly.

Reviewing background information or other research on a similar research topic (Stage 2 on Activity Sheet 2.2)

1. Explain that when the children have a broad idea about what they are interested in investigating, as in Stage 1 on Activity Sheet 2.2, it may be useful to search for some background information in relation to it or look at other research that has already been carried out on a similar topic. This will help them to clarify what they will investigate about their topic. Explain how they may be able to do this, based on Box 2.2.

Box 2.2 Reviewing background information or other research on a topic of interest

For example, if a child is interested in investigating what families in her or his neighbourhood do to preserve the environment, she or he may want to find out if the local council office holds any relevant information. This could be useful to clarify more precisely what the child wants to investigate.

Research on a similar topic or those conducted in a different context or with data from different groups of people might be helpful to review. This will help in forming some ideas about what smaller issues under their wider research topic or question the children might need to pay attention to and/or what their own research process might require them to do.

Some previous research by children can be found on the Internet, in particular, on the websites of university research centres or children's organisations (search for them by using such keywords as 'children's research' and 'research by children'). If appropriate, children can also be directed to search relevant research in academic journals. However, the disadvantage of doing this is that access to research articles in most academic journals requires payment. It may also take considerable time to locate articles relevant to a child's specific topic.

Wrap up

For the children who have not decided their research topic during the session, suggest that they continue to think about it using Activity Sheet 2.2.

Remind the children to put the activity and information sheets from the session into their research folders.

My social research topic checklist

1. Would researching this topic help me to know more about people's thoughts, feelings, behaviours and/or experiences?

2. Would researching this topic require doing more than just looking things up in a book or on the Internet?

3. Would researching this topic find out something 'worth' knowing about? If so, why would it be worth knowing?

4. Can I do the research about this topic by myself, or with my partner(s), and within the length of time that I may have?

5. Does the topic reflect any of my personal biases? (It must not!)

6. Would researching the topic harm anybody in any possible way? (It must not!)

Is this topic or question good for my own social research?

1. How do primary school children across my country feel about taking exams?

2. The opinions of children in my school about doing boring homework

3. What do families in my neighbourhood do to help protect the environment?

4. How many days does it take for a rose bud to bloom?

5. The number of children in my school who like the colour blue

6. How watching a violent film affects pre-school children

Identifying my social research topic

Stage 1. What am I interested in?

Is there anything that you are curious about concerning what people think, feel and/or do at school, where you live or anywhere else?

Stage 2. Review background information or other research on a similar topic

Find out what information is already available in books, on the Internet or elsewhere about what you are interested in.

If it exists, find other research on a similar topic or set in a different context (carried out in a different school, neighbourhood or any other place, or carried out about different groups of people) and see how it was carried out and what it found.

Doing this may help you to think more clearly about what you might like to investigate.

Stage 3. Check what I am interested in against 'My social research topic checklist'

Check what you are interested in investigating against the six criteria on 'My social research topic checklist' and adjust it, if necessary.

If you think it is not possible to adjust what you are interested in to satisfy all the criteria on the checklist, please go back to Stage 1 and start again.

I think my social research topic (or research question) will be:

Three key principles

Be sceptical, be systematic and be ethical

Session objectives

- Know the three key principles in doing social research: be sceptical, be systematic and be ethical
- Understand what being sceptical in social research involves
- Understand what being systematic in social research involves
- Understand what being ethical in social research involves

Key vocabulary

Sceptical, systematic, ethical, research participants, informed consent, confidential, anonymous

Resources

- Copies of Activity Sheets 3.1 and 3.2
- Drawing paper and drawing pencils

Introduction

1. Ask the children what they remember from the activity of comparing a well-organised foreign trip and doing social research in Session 1 (Information Sheet 1.1).
2. Explain that they will now learn something that is equivalent to learning about how to behave abroad throughout the foreign trip.

They will learn how to behave as a researcher: 'be sceptical', 'be systematic' and 'be ethical' (Kellett, 2005).

Be sceptical

1. Ask the children what being 'sceptical' might mean. Then explain that by doing the activity below they will think about what it means.
2. Distribute copies of Activity Sheet 3.1, 'Bread is deadly!' The children read the article on the activity sheet and see what they think.
3. In a plenary, ask them what they think about the article's conclusion and why. Go through each sentence of the article with the children, asking how true it is and why.

Box 3.1 Some tips on reading 'Bread is deadly!'

Most sentences in the article may sound true on the surface, but the fact that they may sound true does not mean that the underlying suggestion – that bread is the main reason behind each of the phenomena in the sentences – is true. For example, the first sentence – most criminals eat bread – may be true, but it does not follow that bread caused criminals to commit crime. Other people who are not criminals also eat bread.

Most sentences in the article are written as if bread is the main cause of what happened. They were used by the author (the person who wrote it) as 'evidence' to support his or her conclusion that bread is deadly. However, they are 'false' evidence.

---

4. Emphasise the following two points to the children:

   Sometimes people say or write what seems to be true at first glance as if it is 'evidence' to support what they claim, as the author did in 'Bread is deadly!' So, when the children read or listen to anything, they need to think carefully about whether each and every thing that the speaker or the writer says is indeed true. This is being 'sceptical'.

   They should not only be sceptical about other people's evidence but they also need to be sceptical about what they collect as evidence in their own research. So, throughout their research process, they need to keep asking themselves the question: 'do my findings really support what they look like they support?'

Be systematic

1. Ask the children what being 'systematic' might mean.

2. Divide the children into small groups and distribute some drawing paper and pencils. The children decide on a type of cake that they would like to bake, draw it on a piece of drawing paper and discuss what they need to do to bake it precisely as they would like it to be.

    Specify the length of time to complete this task. Otherwise the children could spend hours doing it!

3. In a plenary, each group present what they discussed. Then ask the children what might be a good strategy to bake the cake precisely as they would like it to be. Lead the discussion to compare two different strategies:

   a. Having a plan (e.g. drawing the cake with descriptions of all its decorations and what each part of the cake would be made of and preparing a recipe of what to do at each stage of the baking process) and then following it in a step-by-step and precise manner (e.g. the right amounts of ingredients, right temperatures and lengths of time in the oven); or

   b. Trying to bake it without a plan and based on rough ideas in their heads.

   Explain that having a plan and implementing it in a step-by-step and precise manner is being 'systematic'.

4. Discuss with the children, based on Information Sheet 1.2 (the social research process), how they could be systematic in their research process: they will have an overall research plan and carry it out in a step-by-step manner (i.e. one stage after another) and, within each stage, they will also be systematic in what they do.

Be ethical

1. Ask the children what they think being 'ethical' in doing research might mean. Then explain that the people whom they involve in their research are called 'research participants' and being ethical in this case means not harming their research participants in any way.

2. Ask the children whether they remember having discussed before that research must not harm anybody in any possible way. Remind them that the last criterion of 'My social research topic checklist' (Information Sheet 2.1) is about being ethical.

3. Discuss with the children how being involved in research might harm research participants. Lead the discussion based on the examples of the harm that research might cause to its participants, in Box 3.2, which researchers must avoid.

Box 3.2 Examples of possible harm to research participants

- Physical harm: e.g. pain or any other adverse bodily effect which could result from doing things that a researcher asks them to do as part of the research.
- Emotional harm: e.g. anxiety, embarrassment, depression, mistrust as a result of doing things that a researcher asks them to do as part of research, or if their privacy is affected as a result of being involved in research.
- Financial harm: e.g. cost of time or monetary cost for having to travel to take part in research.

(adapted from Kellett, 2005)

 The discussion should start to build the children's understanding of what being ethical in research involves. The following activity seeks to consolidate this understanding.

4. Explain that social researchers normally have their research plan checked by an 'ethics committee' – a group of people who examine whether the planned research is ethical or not – before they start to involve research participants in their research.

 If the children ask who will examine their research plans, explain that the adult facilitator and the other children will take the role.

5. Suggest that in this session, the children play the role of an ethics committee and examine some examples of children's research. Divide the children into small groups and call them 'Ethics Committee A', 'Ethics Committee B', 'Ethics Committee C' and so on. Then distribute copies of Activity Sheet 3.2 with 'Fred's Research' and 'Angie's research'. The children discuss with their fellow committee members whether each child's research was ethical and if so, why it was, and if not, why it was not.

6. In a plenary, the children present what they discussed about 'Fred's research'. Lead the discussion based on Box 3.3. Then talk about how they would change Fred's research for it to be ethical.

Box 3.3 Discussion points about 'Fred's research'

● Fred harmed some children physically, and possibly emotionally too, by asking his friend to barge into them.

● Fred hid from the children that he had set up this barging situation as part of his research. Was it right that Fred did not tell the children what was going to happen to them in advance?

A researcher should not hide anything from her or his research participants and should get their permission first before involving them in their research. This is called getting 'informed consent'. The participants should be fully informed about what they will be asked to do and why before they agree (consent) to take part in the research.

7. The children present what they discussed about 'Angie's research'. Lead the discussion based on Box 3.4.

Box 3.4 Discussion points about 'Angie's research'

● Was it right for Angie to report specifically who said what in the research?

A researcher must not disclose any information that would enable other people to identify who said what in their research, especially if the research participants did not agree to it (by 'informed consent'). This is called being 'confidential' about the information that their research participants gave them.

The researcher can discuss what they found out from the research with other people but they must not reveal any real names. Not revealing any real names and not letting other people be able to tell who gave particular pieces of information is making the research participants 'anonymous'.

- Why must researchers be 'confidential' about the information they collect from their research participants and keep them 'anonymous'?

All research participants' feelings and opinions must be respected. No one should be caused any harm, including emotional harm, by being involved in research.

Researchers need to consider whether anything they do during any of the stages of research might cause harm to any of the research participants.

8. Based on Box 3.5, discuss with the children how Angie in 'Angie's research' could report her findings.

Box 3.5 How could Angie report her findings?

Angie could say that 'eight children from my school received pocket money of less than £2 a week', but she must not say their names. Angie could also say that the reason why the children said they received less than £2 a week was because their parents were poor, but again she must not say who the children were.

Wrap up

Ask the children to explain in their own words what each of the three key principles of doing research means. Ask them to start to think about how they could apply these three principles to their own research.

Bread is deadly!

What do you think about the conclusion of the article below? Why do you think that?

Toasters don't kill people ... but bread is deadly!

Most criminals eat bread.

Most violent crimes are committed within a few hours of eating bread.

About 300 years ago, when almost all bread was baked at home, many babies died before their first birthday.

Bread is made from a substance called 'dough' and it has been proven that as little as one pound of dough can be used to suffocate a mouse.

New-born babies can choke on bread.

Bread is baked in the oven at high temperatures and this level of heat can kill an adult in less than one minute.

So, bread is deadly!

For the ethics committee's evaluation

Was Fred's and Angie's research ethical? If so, why was it? If not, why was it not?

Fred's research

Fred was curious about how children in his neighbourhood might feel about being barged into by other children, and how they might react to it. In order to investigate this, he asked his best friend to barge into some children in the park so that he could see how these children reacted.

Later Fred also asked the children how they felt when they were barged into. In doing these things Fred did not tell the children that he had asked his friend to barge into them as part of his research. This was because he wanted to observe their natural reactions.

Angie's research

Angie wanted to find out how much children in her school thought was good to receive as pocket money each week and why they thought this. In order to investigate it, she asked 80 children from her school several questions about their pocket money. The questions included: 'how much pocket money do you get each week?', 'why do you think your parents give you that amount of money?', 'how much pocket money would you like to get each week?', 'why would you like to receive this amount?' and so on.

Among her research participants, eight children, including Felix and Emma, said they received less than £2 a week and this was because their parents were poor. Angie found it surprising that some children received less than £2 a week and, when reporting her findings, she wrote that Felix and Emma received less than £2 a week and it was because their parents were poor.

Data collection method one
Questionnaires

Session objectives

- Know the characteristics of open-ended and closed questions and the differences between them
- Know the different types of answer choices for closed questions
- Know how to design a questionnaire
- Understand the need for piloting a questionnaire
- Understand the advantages and disadvantages of using a questionnaire for collecting data
- Understand the ethical issues associated with using a questionnaire

Key vocabulary

Questionnaire, open-ended question, closed question, piloting

Resources

- Copies of Activity Sheets 4.1 to 4.4, and Information Sheets 4.1 and 4.2
- Some sticky notes or a whiteboard

Introduction

1. As a review of Session 3, ask the children what the three key principles of doing research are and to explain in their own words what each of them means.

2. Explain to the children that in the next few sessions they will learn several different methods that researchers use most frequently to collect data. These are questionnaires, interviews, observations and using visual materials. Throughout these sessions, the children should think about which of these methods would be most useful for their own research.

 The most important thing to consider in deciding the data collection method is which one will generate the kind of data that will best help the children investigate their research topic or question. If necessary, they may decide to use more than one method.

Identifying what to ask on a questionnaire

1. Ask the children whether they have seen a questionnaire and then what a researcher might do with it when collecting data.

    Show the children the sample questionnaire on Activity Sheet 4.4 (however, do not distribute the activity sheet yet).

Box 4.1 A questionnaire is ...

A 'questionnaire' is a piece of paper with all the questions that the researcher needs to ask her or his research participants written on it. The researcher gives this to the research participants to write their answers on.

A questionnaire can also be created and sent to the research participants using online programs that are available on the Internet.

---

2. Discuss with them what the first thing to do might be when making a questionnaire.

    Researchers first need to identify a list of things that they want to find out using the questionnaire in order to investigate the research topic fully.

3. Taking an example of a research question, 'do children in my school want to go to university and why?', ask the children what they might like to find out in order to address this research question fully. Put the children's suggestions on sticky notes or on the whiteboard.

For the adult facilitator's reference, Activity Sheet 4.3 provides an example list of things that a researcher might want to find out about the research question.

Types of question and answer choices

1. Explain that the children need to form questions carefully to make sure that they find out precisely the things they want to know about. They will now learn about the types of questions that researchers usually use on a questionnaire.

    Broadly, there are two different types of questions they can ask on a questionnaire: 'open-ended' questions and 'closed' questions. Ask the children what they think 'open-ended' and 'closed' questions are before explaining them as in Box 4.2.

Box 4.2 Open-ended and closed questions

'Open-ended' questions let research participants give any answers they want to. For this reason, answers to these questions can be much longer than answers to closed questions. For example, 'what do you think of our school playground?'

'Closed' questions ask research participants to choose from a set of answer choices that they are given. For example, for the question 'is it important to be liked by your teacher?', 'yes' or 'no' may be given as the answer choices from which to choose.

---

2. Distribute copies of Activity Sheet 4.1. Ask the children whether each of the questions on the activity sheet is an open-ended question or a closed question (some of the questions are in the form of a statement).

    Questions 4 and 6 on the activity sheet are open-ended questions and the rest of the questions are closed questions. However, questions 3 and 7 also contain some element of an open-ended question in order to capture research participants' answers fully, which may not have been included in the given answer choices.

3. Go through each closed question on Activity Sheet 4.1 to help the children understand the different types of answer choices, based on the points in Box 4.3.

Box 4.3 Types of answer choices for closed questions in Activity Sheet 4.1

- 'Yes' or 'No' as in questions 1 and 3.
- Categories as in questions 2, 5, 7 and 10.
- Answer choices on a rating scale as in questions 8 and 9.

Depending on the question or the statement, research participants can be asked to indicate, for example, a degree of importance (as in question 8), or a degree of agreement (how much they agree with it as in question 9).

   In the examples, five levels or points are given but rating scales can give fewer or more levels or points to choose from. However, and especially when a degree of agreement is being asked for, the levels or points are usually given in an odd number with the middle point to indicate that research participants neither agree nor disagree with the statement or question.

4. Discuss with the children how they might decide what type of question to use. Lead the discussion based on Box 4.4.

Box 4.4 Deciding between open-ended questions and closed questions

The choice of which type of question to use will depend on what type of answers are helpful for the researcher to investigate a particular issue concerning their research topic. When designing questions, the researcher also needs to think about how they will analyse the answers to the questions later on (the children will learn in later sessions how they will analyse data including those collected using a questionnaire).

   If the researcher wants to know what their research participants think in detail, it may be better to use an open-ended question. For example, if she or he wants to know why some people do not like physical education, some research participants may not find the most suitable reason for them among the answer choices to a closed question. In comparison, an open-ended question will allow them to write down their own reasons and in detail.

However, answers to open-ended questions tend to be longer and much less predictable than those to closed questions, so they may be less straightforward to analyse. Answers to closed questions can be counted easily because the answer choices are fixed. For example, the researcher can count how many children chose each of the answer choices for the closed questions on Activity Sheet 4.1.

A good question and a bad question

Distribute copies of Activity Sheet 4.2. Ask the children to think about (a) why each question might be a bad question, and (b) how it can be changed into a good question. The children can do this activity in pairs or individually.

Suggested answers for Activity Sheet 4.2

Question 1: 'Carrot' is not a fruit and furthermore research participants who do not like any of the suggested kinds of fruit cannot answer the question accurately. This question may be better as an open-ended question because children's favourite fruit may vary so much that it is not possible to list all of them as answer choices.

Question 2: The answer choices are vague because the meaning of 'often' can vary greatly from person to person. The answer choices should be changed to, for example, 'almost every day', 'five or six times a week', 'three or four times a week', 'once or twice a week', 'less than once a week' and 'never'.

Question 3: This question is asking more than one thing. This can be confusing to the research participants and also makes it difficult for the researcher to analyse answers to the question. It would be better to break it into two separate questions. Stress to the children that in a questionnaire, questions should only ask one thing at a time!

Question 4: Answers to this question are likely to be very short, being either 'yes' or 'no', so although it is an open-ended question, the researcher will not get much extra information by using it. It is also vague what 'tall' means. If the researcher wants to find out the range of heights that their research participants fall into, they should use a closed question with different ranges of height to choose from, for example, 'less than 120 cm', 'from 120 cm to less than 130 cm', 'from 130 cm to less than 140 cm', '140 cm or taller', and so on.

Question 5: The tone of the sentence can cause research participants to form a biased opinion about the school toilets, which may affect their answers to the question. It would be better to change the question to 'I would like to change the colour of our school toilets'.

Designing a questionnaire

Distribute copies of Activity Sheet 4.3. The children design a questionnaire individually as asked on the activity sheet.

 The adult facilitator should specify the length of time for the children to do this activity, for example, 15 or 20 minutes, unless a longer time is available. Most children would require more time to complete their questionnaires. The following activity on piloting a questionnaire can be carried out with the few questions that the children will have managed to produce within the time allowed.

Piloting a questionnaire

1. Explain that before using a questionnaire with their research participants, it is helpful to test it first. This can be done with a small number of people who are similar to their research participants in terms of the characteristics that can be significant to their research topic such as age and gender (for example, if the research is about primary school children, testing it with a few adults may not be very helpful). This is called 'piloting' the questionnaire.

   Discuss with the children why it might be useful to do this, based on Box 4.5.

Box 4.5 Why pilot a questionnaire?

Piloting a questionnaire is to see whether the questionnaire works as the researcher expected when she or he was designing it. The researcher can tell, for example:

- Whether the research participants can understand the questions accurately or the questions may be unclear

- Whether the questions ask what they are supposed to ask (in other words, whether the questions prompt the research participants to give the kinds of information that they were designed to be about)
- Whether the researcher needs to include some more questions or delete some which do not seem to provide any useful information.

The researcher can also find out how long it may take to complete the questionnaire.

2. In order to practise 'piloting', the children exchange their questionnaires with each other and fill them in. Ask them what they think about the questionnaire that they have just filled in.

3. After this, let them return the questionnaires to the children who designed them. Ask the children to examine the answers that were given on their questionnaires and then consider the following questions with them:
   - Were the questions understood accurately by the children who answered them?
   - Did they get the type of information that they wanted from the questions?
   - In the case of open-ended questions, did they get as much information as they wanted?
   Explain that the children can use such feedback to improve their questionnaire before actually using it with their research participants.

Ethics when designing a questionnaire

1. Ask if the children can remember what 'informed consent', 'anonymity' and 'confidentiality' mean. Discuss with them how these ethical principles might be relevant to using a questionnaire for data collection.

   Explain that when they make a questionnaire, there are two things that they need to let their research participants know before asking them to fill it in, as in Box 4.6.

> ## Box 4.6 Two things to do in order to make a questionnaire ethical
>
> - Briefly explain what the research is about in order to help the research participants understand why they are being asked to fill in the questionnaire. This is for 'informed consent'.
> - Even if the research participants are asked not to write their names on the questionnaire, assure them that when reporting findings from the questionnaire, the researcher will keep them 'anonymous' and that all their answers will remain 'confidential'.

2. Distribute copies of Activity Sheet 4.4, with a sample questionnaire for the research question of 'do children in my school want to go to university and why?' Discuss with the children how the sample questionnaire addresses the ethical principles.

3. Distribute copies of Information Sheet 4.1, 'Checklist for designing a questionnaire', and briefly go through the checklist with the children.

   Ask the children to evaluate the sample questionnaire on Activity Sheet 4.4 against the checklist when they get home or outside the session (if time allows, this could be done during the session). It is also suggested that the children think about how they might have designed the questionnaire on Activity Sheet 4.4 differently.

 Activity Sheet 4.4 asks the children how they might design the questionnaire differently in order to encourage them to see it as only a sample and to help them think critically and creatively, if they plan to use a questionnaire for their research.

Advantages and disadvantages of using a questionnaire

Discuss with the children what they think the advantages and disadvantages may be of using a questionnaire. Then distribute Information Sheet 4.2 and go through the table with them.

Wrap up

Discuss with the children whether they think using a questionnaire might be good for their own research and the reasons why they think this.

Examples of questions for a questionnaire

1. Please tick as appropriate: I am a member of the school council.

   Yes ☐   No ☐

2. Please tick as appropriate:

   I am   Female ☐   Male ☐

3. Please tick your answer: Do you own a pet animal?

   Yes ☐   No ☐

   If your answer is 'yes', please specify what animal it is _____

   _____

4. How do you feel about the amount of homework that you receive? Please write your answer as fully as possible below.

5. Please tick your answer: How many brothers and/or sisters do you have?

   None ☐   One ☐   Two ☐   Three ☐   More than three ☐

6. What do you think about children earning their pocket money? Please write your answer as fully as possible below.

7. Please tick your answer: What is your favourite sport?

Swimming ☐   Football ☐   Tennis ☐   Cricket ☐   Other ☐

None (I don't like sport) ☐   If other, please specify: _____

_____

8. Please tick your answer: How important is it to feel liked by your teacher?

Very important ☐   Fairly important ☐   Important ☐

Slightly important ☐   Not at all important ☐

9. Please tick your answer: Our school council represents the opinions of the children in our school.

Strongly agree ☐   Agree ☐   Neither agree nor disagree ☐

Disagree ☐   Strongly disagree ☐

10. Please tick your answer: How often do you exercise a week?

Six to seven times a week ☐   Three to five times a week ☐

Once or twice a week ☐   Less than once a week ☐   Never ☐

Designing questions for a questionnaire: bad questions?

Think about why each question below might be a bad question and how you could turn it into a good question.

1. What is your favourite fruit?

   Apple ☐　Banana ☐　Melon ☐　Carrot ☐　Strawberry ☐

2. How often do you play video games?

   Very often ☐　Quite often ☐　Not very often ☐

3. What do you think about our school playground and what do you think about our school toilets?

4. Are you tall?

5. Please tick what you think about the following sentence: I would like to change the colour of our smelly school toilets.

   Agree ☐　Neither agree nor disagree ☐　Disagree ☐

Identifying and designing questions for a questionnaire

In order to help investigate the research question 'do children in my school want to go to university and why?', Michael, a child researcher, identified the following list of things that he wanted to find out. Design a questionnaire that will enable him to find them out. If you think he needs to add some other things to the list in order to investigate his research question more fully, please include them in your questionnaire.

- What proportion of the children in my school know what a university is?
- For the children who know what a university is, how did they get to know what it is?
- What proportion of the children in my school want to go to university?
- For the children who want to go to university, what are their reasons?
- For the children who want to go to university, what do they want to study there?
- For the children who want to go to university, how important is it for them to do so?
- For the children who do not want to go to university, what are their reasons?
- What do the children think the advantages of going to university are?
- What do the children think the disadvantages of going to university are?
- What the answers are from children in each year group to the above list of questions
- What the answers are from the boys and the girls in the school, respectively, to the above list of questions

The following questionnaire was made by a child researcher, Michael, to investigate the research question of 'do children in my school want to go to university and why?' If you were doing a similar research project, how might you have written it differently, for example, by adding some questions, deleting others or wording some of the questions differently?

Questionnaire

Do children in my school want to go to university and why?

Hello. I am Michael. I am investigating whether children in our school want to go to university and the reasons for their thoughts. Your participation in filling in this questionnaire will help me a lot in this investigation. Completing the questionnaire will take about five to ten minutes.

In answering this questionnaire, please do not write your name. This is to keep who you are unknown to me as well as to the people to whom I will report findings from my investigation.

If there is any question that you do not understand, please do not hesitate to contact me. When you have finished filling it in, please insert it in the box that I set up for the collection of the questionnaires at the school reception. Thank you very much for your help.

1. Please tick as appropriate. I am: Female ☐   Male ☐

2. What year are you in (for example, Year 3, Year 5 …)?

3. Do you know what a university is?   Yes ☐   No ☐

    If your answer to the above question is 'yes', how did you get to know what it is? Please tick as appropriate.

    Talk with parents ☐   Talk with relatives ☐

    Heard about it at school ☐   Don't remember ☐   Other ☐

    If your answer to the above question is 'other', please specify below how you got to know what a university is.

4. Do you want to go to university?   Yes ☐   No ☐

   If your answer to the above question is 'yes', please give your reasons why you want to go as fully as possible. If your answer is 'no', please give your reasons why you do not want to go as fully as possible.

5. If you want to go to university, what do you want to study there?

6. If you want to go to university, how important is it for you to be able to do so?

   Very important ☐   Important ☐   A little important ☐   Not important ☐

7. What do you think the advantages are of going to university? Please write your answer as fully as possible.

8. What do you think the disadvantages are of going to university? Please write your answer as fully as possible.

Thank you for completing this questionnaire. Please insert the questionnaire in the box set up for its collection at the school reception.

Checklist for designing a questionnaire

1. Have I included a sentence or two that explains to my research participants what my research is about?

2. Have I explained that my research participants will be 'anonymous' and their answers will be 'confidential'?

3. If I am not collecting the questionnaire back from my research participants immediately after they have filled it in, have I explained clearly how they can return it?

4. Have I thanked my research participants for taking the time to fill in the questionnaire?

5. Have I given clear instructions on how to answer each question (for example, 'tick one box only', 'tick as many boxes as are relevant to you' or 'please write your answer as fully as possible')?

6. Will answers to each question help me to answer my research question or investigate my research topic?

7. Are all my questions clear and easy to understand?

8. If it is a closed question, are the answer choices sufficient and suitable?

9. If it is a closed question, are all the answer choices clear and easy to understand?

10. Have I asked only one question at a time?

11. Have I used any words that may reflect my own opinions, which may influence my research participants' answers to the question? (I must not!)

Advantages and disadvantages of using a questionnaire

Advantages	Disadvantages
It can be used to collect data from a large number of research participants in a relatively short time.	It is difficult to use with people who cannot read or write, such as very young children.
Because a questionnaire does not usually ask research participants to write their names, they may feel more comfortable about giving honest answers than if the researcher asks them in person. (Although research participants might feel more comfortable about giving honest answers if they do not write their names on the questionnaire, there is still a chance that they may not be entirely honest.)	If the researcher gives copies of a questionnaire to research participants to fill in by themselves and return to her or him later, not all of them may do so. The 'response rate' of questionnaires is usually not very high.

Data collection method two

Interviews

Session objectives

- Know the characteristics of 'structured', 'semi-structured' and 'unstructured' interviews
- Be able to design a semi-structured interview schedule
- Understand the practical issues of conducting interviews
- Know how using interviews is different from using a questionnaire
- Understand the advantages and disadvantages of interviews for collecting data
- Understand the ethical issues associated with conducting interviews

Key vocabulary

Structured interview, semi-structured interview, unstructured interview, interview schedule, probing questions, transcribe, transcript

Resources

- Copies of Activity Sheets 5.1 and 5.2, and Information Sheets 5.1 and 5.2
- Copies of a sample transcript of an interview

Introduction

1. To review Session 4 on questionnaires, discuss with the children the advantages and disadvantages of using questionnaires for collecting data.

2. Ask the children what interviews, as a way of collecting data, may involve and then what the advantages of using interviews might be, compared with using questionnaires. Lead the discussion based on Box 5.1.

Box 5.1 Interviews and their advantages

Interviews involve asking research participants questions face to face. An advantage of interviews is that the researcher can use them with people who cannot read and/or write. Furthermore, since interviews collect data directly from research participants, there is not the problem about whether the questionnaires are returned to the researcher.

---

3. Explain that in this session, they will learn how to plan and conduct interviews and suggest that, while they are doing this, they think about what other advantages and also disadvantages there might be in using interviews to collect data.

Types of interviews: 'structured', 'semi-structured' and 'unstructured'

1. Explain that there are broadly three types of interviews: 'structured', 'semi-structured' and 'unstructured'. Ask the children if they can guess what each type of interview might be like, based on the names: each type of interview varies according to how much it is 'structured'.

 When using interviews, research participants can also be called 'interviewees' (the persons who are interviewed), and the researcher or the person who conducts the interviews can be called an 'interviewer'.

Structured interview

Ask the children how a 'structured' interview might be carried out. Lead the discussion based on Box 5.2.

Box 5.2 Structured interviews

- A structured interview is similar to a questionnaire, except that the researcher reads out the questions to the research participants.
- Just as they must design a questionnaire before giving it out to their research participants, researchers must design an 'interview schedule' before conducting an interview. The 'interview schedule' for a structured interview will look very much like a questionnaire.
- As with a questionnaire, a structured interview schedule can have both 'closed' and 'open-ended' questions. However, a structured interview schedule will tend to contain more 'closed' than 'open-ended' questions.

Semi-structured interview

Distribute copies of Activity Sheet 5.1. Ask the children, based on the sample semi-structured interview schedule, how a semi-structured interview might be different from a structured interview. Lead the discussion based on Box 5.3.

Box 5.3 Structured interviews and semi-structured interviews

- For a structured interview, the interviewer sticks to what they had planned to ask in their interview schedule throughout the interview. They just read out the questions from the page and nothing else.
- In comparison, for a semi-structured interview, the interviewer asks all the interviewees the same list of questions but, in addition to this, if they hear something that they want to find out about in more detail in the interviewees' answers, they can also ask some further questions in response. These are usually called 'probing questions'.

- A semi-structured interview schedule usually has a list of open-ended questions. For each of these questions it may also have a list of possible probing questions that the interviewer could ask, depending on the interviewees' answers to a given question. However, probing questions are often thought of on the spot during each interview.

The sample semi-structured interview schedule on Activity Sheet 5.1 includes things to do in order to address ethical issues at the beginning of the interview. In social research, an interview requires a relevant consent form to be signed by the interviewee in advance. Issues about consent forms are introduced in Session 6. Even if a consent form has been signed before the interview, the researcher may still mention these ethical issues as a reminder to the interviewee. The adult facilitator may clarify this point in Session 6.

Unstructured interview

Ask the children how an 'unstructured' interview might differ from 'structured' and 'semi-structured' interviews. Lead the discussion based on Box 5.4.

Box 5.4 Unstructured interviews

How are unstructured interviews conducted?

Unstructured interviews are used when the researcher does not wish to influence the interviewees' answers by asking them specific questions as in structured and semi-structured interviews.

When conducting an unstructured interview, the researcher may start with a conversational question or suggest a topic to talk about (for example, 'what do you think about our school toilets?' or 'shall we talk about our school toilets?'). The researcher then lets the interviewee speak freely about whatever they want to on the topic. While doing so, the researcher can ask probing questions occasionally and when appropriate.

The advantage of unstructured interviews

Because it allows them to speak freely and in detail about a given topic, an unstructured interview can get a lot of details about how the interviewees think and feel about the particular aspects of the topic that they think are important.

The disadvantage of unstructured interviews

For any topic, each interviewee may want to talk about very different things, so it is usually very difficult to compare the data gathered from different interviews. For example, one interviewee may talk about how she dislikes the smell from the school toilets and relates everything that she says about the toilets to the smell issues; another interviewee may focus on the number of toilets and any issues that arise from this; and other interviewees may focus on the behaviour of the children in the toilets.

Differentiating between structured, semi-structured and unstructured interviews

Distribute Activity Sheet 5.2. The children decide which interview type each statement on it describes.

 Statements 1, 3, 5 and 7 are structured interviews while statements 2 and 6 are semi-structured interviews, and statement 4 is unstructured interviews.

Checklist for designing a semi-structured interview schedule

Distribute Information Sheet 5.1, 'Checklist for designing a semi-structured interview schedule'. Go through the checklist with the children. If time allows, using the checklist, ask the children to assess the sample semi-structured interview schedule in Activity Sheet 5.1.

 The adult facilitator may remind the children that a structured interview schedule is similar to a questionnaire so that they can use the checklist for designing a questionnaire, while an unstructured interview does not really require an interview schedule.

Piloting an interview schedule and practising interview skills

1. Ask the children what they did in the session on questionnaires to test whether their questionnaire would work as they anticipated. They 'piloted' it and they need to do the same with their interview schedule to see whether it works as they planned. Discuss with the children how piloting, in particular, a semi-structured interview schedule might be similar to, or different from, piloting a questionnaire. Lead the discussion based on Box 5.5.

Box 5.5 Piloting a semi-structured interview schedule

The children will ask the interview questions face to face, so they need to see whether they are able to ask the questions clearly and also whether they can think of good probing questions at appropriate times. Based on the answers that they get during the piloting, they can think of some possible probing questions that they might ask during the actual interviews.

When piloting an interview schedule, they need to check roughly how long it takes to complete, so that they can inform their research participants in advance.

 Before asking the children to practise piloting a semi-structured interview schedule, the adult facilitator might wish to demonstrate first how to do it.

2. In pairs, the children pilot the semi-structured interview schedule on Activity Sheet 5.1 on each other in turn. Then, in a plenary, discuss with the children the questions in Table 5.1.

Table 5.1 Questions to children as interviewers and as interviewees

Children as interviewers	*Children as interviewees*
Did the interview go as they planned?	Could they understand all the questions clearly?
If the answer to the above question is 'no', what, in particular, did not go as they planned?	What did they think about the way the interviewer asked the questions?
How could they improve it (e.g. modify the interview schedule, improve their interview skills)?	How might the interviewer improve their interview skills?

Non-verbal interview data

1. If the children do not pick out issues to do with non-verbal communication between the interviewer and the interviewee during the above activity, ask the children whether there might be other ways of guessing what the interviewee might be thinking and feeling.

2. Explain that they might be able to guess what their interviewees might be thinking or feeling by their facial expressions and body language – for example, whether they approve or disapprove of something, whether they are enthusiastic about what is being asked or whether they are bored with it. Give the children the example in Box 5.6.

Box 5.6 An example of non-verbal interview data

To the question 'are you satisfied with how clean our school toilets are?', an interviewee answers 'yes' with a shrug. How would the interviewer interpret this gesture? The interviewer might want to ask a probing question to check the interviewee's answer, such as 'are you always satisfied with it or are there times when you are not?'

Managing interview data

1. Activity Sheet 5.1 introduced the idea of taking notes or using an audio recorder to record interview data. Referring back to Activity Sheet 5.1, lead a discussion on recording interview data based on Box 5.7.

Box 5.7 Recording interview data: 'transcribe' and 'transcript'

Researchers can take notes of their interviewees' answers, but a more accurate way of recording interview data might be to audio-record or video-record it. If a researcher audio-records or video-records interviews, they usually 'transcribe' the recordings. 'Transcribe' is to put speech or verbal data into a written form (i.e. the interview is typed up). A written version of an interview is called a 'transcript'.

2. Distribute copies of a sample interview transcript. Discuss the advantages of having transcripts and other things to know about audio-recording interviews, based on Box 5.8.

Box 5.8 Interview transcripts and audio-recording interviews

Advantages of having interview transcripts

- Transcripts help researchers to remember what was said by interviewees and help them to analyse the interview data more easily and accurately.

- When reporting their research findings, researchers can use direct quotes from the interviewees – a few phrases or sentences from the transcripts – in order to give readers a vivid description of what the interviewees actually said.

More things to know about audio-recording interviews

- Audio recordings do not record interviewees' facial expressions and gestures or other things that they cannot capture. So, it is always a good idea to make written notes about how the interviews went in addition to audio-recording them.

- It usually takes a long time to transcribe an interview (for example, it can take about 50 to 60 minutes to transcribe a 10-minute interview recording).

Advantages and disadvantages of interviews

1. Ask the children what advantages and disadvantages interviews might have compared with using questionnaires. Lead the discussion based on Information Sheet 5.2 and then distribute the copies of the information sheet.

2. Referring back to Activity Sheet 5.1, discuss with the children whether using a questionnaire instead of semi-structured interviews might be more useful for investigating the research question on the activity sheet.

Wrap up

Ask the children to think about: (a) whether using a questionnaire or interviews will be useful for their own research projects; (b) whether using both methods might be better for their projects; or (c) whether neither of the methods seems useful and they think they might need some other type of data.

A semi-structured interview schedule

Emily designed the following semi-structured interview schedule to investigate the research question 'what do children in my year group think about behaviour during lessons?' If you were doing a similar research project, how might you design the semi-structured interview schedule differently? For example, would adding some other questions be helpful for investigating the research question, or might wording some of the questions differently help to get more useful data?

Before asking questions

- Introduce myself to the interviewee and thank her or him for giving up their time for the interview.

- Explain what the interview is for ('*I am interested in finding out what children in our year group think about behaviour during lessons. This interview will help me to investigate it*').

- Explain that I will keep any notes from, or the recording of, this interview secure in a locked place so that no one can access it and, when reporting findings from the research, I will keep them 'anonymous'.

- Explain that if there is any question that they do not wish to answer, they can say so and at any point of the interview, if they do not wish to continue, they may leave.

- If the interviewee does not want the interview to be audio-recorded, I need to make notes of the interviewee's answers.

Questions

1. Note whether the interviewee is female or male.

2. Note which class of our year group the interviewee is in.

3. What do you think about behaviour during lessons?
   - If the answer to the above question is 'so-so', 'good' or 'very good', ask 'do you notice any bad behaviour during lessons?' (If the answer to this question is 'yes', then say 'please give me some examples of bad behaviour'.)
   - If the answer to the above question is 'bad' or 'very bad', say 'please give me examples of bad and/or very bad behaviour'.

4. Does bad behaviour during lessons affect your learning?
   - If the answer to the above question is 'yes', ask 'in what ways does it affect your learning?' and then, 'how much does it affect your learning (e.g. a lot, quite a lot, a little)?'

5. Why do you think children behave badly during lessons? (Depending on the answers, ask some probing questions.)

6. Do you think the teacher manages bad behaviour well?
   - If the answer to the above question is 'yes', then ask 'what does she or he do to manage bad behaviour?'
   - If the answer to the above question is 'no', ask 'why do you think she or he does not manage bad behaviour well?' and then ask, 'what do you think she or he could do instead to manage bad behaviour?'

7. What do you think you can do about bad behaviour? (Depending on the answers, ask 'how can you do it?')

Before finishing the interview

Ask the interviewee: (a) whether they have anything else that they might want to say about my research question, and then (b) whether they have any questions or concerns about the interview.

Thank the interviewee.

Which type of interviews are these?

Decide whether each of the statements below describes a structured, semi-structured or unstructured interview.

1. The researcher does not ask any probing questions at all.

2. The researcher asks all the interviewees the same list of questions and, depending on the interviewees' answers, some probing questions.

3. All the research participants are asked only the questions on the interview schedule.

4. It is the most complicated interview type for comparing interviewees' answers.

5. Of the three types of interviews, it is the easiest to count and compare the interviewees' answers.

6. A majority of the interviewees' answers from this type of interview can be compared, but not all of them.

7. This one is the most similar to using a questionnaire.

Checklist for designing a semi-structured interview schedule

1. Have I included a sentence or two to explain to my interviewees what my research is about?

2. Have I included a statement to tell my interviewees that they will be 'anonymous' and that their answers will be 'confidential'?

3. Have I included a note to ask for the interviewee's permission to audio-record the interview?

4. Will answers to each question help me to know more about my research topic or research question?

5. Have I missed any question that may help me to investigate my research topic or research question fully?

6. Am I asking only one question at a time?

7. Are all my questions clear and easy to understand?

8. If I have included any closed questions, are the answer choices sufficient and suitable for each question?

9. Have I used any words that reflect my own opinions, which might influence how the interviewees answer the questions? (I must not!)

10. Have I included any questions that might upset some of my interviewees? (I must not!)

11. Have I included a note to thank my interviewees for taking the time to participate in my research?

Advantages and disadvantages of using interviews

Advantages	Disadvantages
Interviews can be used with people who cannot read and/or write.	Doing an interview takes a relatively long time, so it is difficult to collect data from a large number of research participants.
Except for structured interviews, researchers can ask probing questions to get more detailed answers.	Because of the researcher's presence, interviewees may not feel comfortable about saying exactly what they think or feel about what they are being asked.
	Except for those produced through structured interviews, the data from one interview tend to come in a large amount and may take a lot of time to transcribe.

A sample transcript of an interview

Research question: what do children in my school worry about?
Interview conducted on 2 June 2015. The interviewee's name has been changed to keep him anonymous.

Interviewer: Matt, thanks again for agreeing to talk to me.

Matt: That's okay.

Interviewer: I told you that I am investigating what children in my school worry about. I will now ask you some questions about it.

Matt: Yeah.

Interviewer: How often do you worry?

Matt: Sometimes.

Interviewer: Hmm, sometimes seems a little vague to me. Please can you say how many times or days you get to worry a week or a month?

Matt: About three or four times a month.

Interviewer: Once you worry about something, how long do the worries last for?

Matt: It depends on what I worry about ...

Interviewer: What do you worry about?

Matt: Different things ...

Interviewer: Please can you give me some examples?

Matt: Yeah. Exams, getting teased by other children, my sister being ill ...

Interviewer: Do you get worried about exams all the time?

Matt: No, not really. But I get worried when I do not have much time to revise.

Interviewer: You want to do well in exams?

Matt: Yes, of course. My parents have a lot of things to care about at the moment, my sister has been ill quite often this year as well ... So, I don't want to be another thing for them to worry about.

Interviewer: Your sister has been ill?

Matt: Yeah. She has been ill for quite some time. But sometimes she gets worse, then we, my parents and I all get worried about her.

Interviewer: I am really sorry about your sister.

Matt: Thanks.

Interviewer: Is that what worries you the most? Or exams, or being teased by other children?

Matt: Being teased by other children is really annoying. But, my sister's health worries me the most.

Interviewer: When you are worried, what do you do about it?

Matt: Hmm, nothing really ... I just hope she gets better ... nothing ... When she recovers a bit, then I get relieved.

Interviewer: ... I hope she becomes healthy soon.

Matt: Yeah.

Interviewer: What about other worries? What do you do about them? Worries about exams?

Matt: Well, I usually get on my bike for a ride around the park and then I feel better. I think to myself that I will revise more next time.

Interviewer: What about being teased by other children? What do you do about it? Do you tell anyone about it?

Matt: Hmm, I sometimes speak about it with my parents. But not all the time especially when my sister needs their attention ...

Interviewer: Do you have anyone else to talk to about it?

Matt: Yeah, my uncle. I don't get to see him very often though. He lives in Yorkshire. I speak with him on the phone. He is a primary school teacher.

Interviewer: Ah, I see. Is it helpful to speak with him?

Matt: Oh, yes, he gives me advice.

Interviewer: What advice does he give you, may I ask?

Matt: What other people talk about you is often not very important ... as long as I keep my own integrity, hardly anything will affect me much.

Interviewer: Thank you Matt. Do you have anything else to tell me about your worries?

Matt: No, not really.

Interviewer: Thank you again for speaking to me for my research.

Matt: That's okay.

Further data collection methods
Observations and using visual materials

Session objectives

- Know the characteristics of different types of observation
- Know how to record an observation
- Understand the advantages and disadvantages of using observation when collecting data
- Understand the ethical issues associated with conducting observation
- Know about the different uses of visual materials in social research
- Understand the advantages and disadvantages of using visual materials when collecting data
- Understand the ethical issues associated with using visual materials

Key vocabulary

Structured observation, unstructured observation, observation schedule, visual materials, consent form

Resources

- Copies of Activity Sheets 6.1 and 6.2, and Information Sheets 6.1 and 6.2
- Copies of the sample consent forms

Introduction

1. To review the two previous data collection methods sessions, discuss with the children the advantages and disadvantages of using questionnaires and interviews.

2. Ask the children whether they can think of any other ways of collecting data for their research.

   Explain that in this session they will learn about: (a) observation (watching how research participants behave or what happens to them); and (b) how they might use 'visual' materials such as photographs, drawings or maps in their research.

What is observation?

1. Ask the children 'if you are interested in how a teacher in a class interacts with her or his pupils, what data would you need and how would you collect them?'

2. Discuss with the children whether asking the teacher and pupils questions about class interactions would be sufficient.

   Observing how the teacher actually interacts with the pupils may be useful. This is because there may be things that the teacher does but is unaware of during the class. Lead the discussion based on Box 6.1.

Box 6.1 Observation

If a researcher is interested in comparing how teachers interact with their pupils, the researcher will need to observe several different teachers teaching their pupils. Or, if the researcher is interested in how one teacher interacts differently with her or his pupils when teaching different subjects, then they will need to observe the teacher teaching different subjects.

Types of observation: 'structured' and 'unstructured'

1. There are broadly two different types of observation. Ask the children what types of observation they might be. The children might guess that, based on their knowledge of questionnaires and interviews, observation can also either be 'structured' or 'unstructured'.

2. Ask the children how they might carry out 'structured' observation. Distribute copies of Activity Sheet 6.1 with 'A sample observation schedule' and lead the discussion based on Box 6.2.

Box 6.2 Conducting structured observation

- When carrying out structured observation, researchers use an observation schedule like the sample on Activity Sheet 6.1 (the researcher who created the sample was interested in how a teacher interacts with the pupils in her class).

- As shown on the sample observation schedule, when recording observation, researchers need to record the date, time, place and any other information that may be useful for analysing the data later on.

- Depending on what is being investigated, researchers decide the length of their observation sessions – for example, the entire lesson, or the first 15 minutes or last 20 minutes of a lesson. If the researcher is interested in how a teacher starts her class, they may observe the first several minutes of her classes.

- In the sample observation schedule, the time unit for observation is five minutes. However, the time units can be shorter or longer depending on what the researcher would like to find out in relation to their research topic. For example, if the researcher wants to find out how early a teacher starts to question individual children and/or how often she questions individual children, it might be useful to have short units of observation for which they check whether, and/or how many times, the particular questioning instance occurred.

- Researchers design their structured observation schedule after deciding: what specific behaviours or events they would like to look for; how long each observation session will be; and how long each time unit within the observation session will be.

---

3. Ask the children how they might carry out 'unstructured' observation. Explain unstructured observation using the example in Box 6.3.

> ## Box 6.3 Conducting unstructured observation: an example
>
> A researcher is interested in the behaviour of children in her school playground. She thinks observing children in the playground during break times will be useful. However, she does not yet know what to look for when she is observing them. So she goes to the playground and records whatever appears to be important to her research topic. She does this for all the break times from Monday to Friday. She writes detailed observation notes for each of these observation sessions, with the date, time and location (where she was in the playground) of the observation.

4. Distribute copies of Information Sheet 6.1 on 'structured' and 'unstructured' observation, and go through their characteristics with the children.

Practising structured observation

Using (a) classroom observation video(s) uploaded on a video-sharing website and Activity Sheet 6.1, the adult facilitator can help the children to practise a structured observation. Alternatively, the adult facilitator may wish to video-record an event that may be more closely relevant to the children and use it for this activity. In order to do this, the adult facilitator will also need to design a sample structured observation schedule to go with it or they can design it with the children.

1. The children carry out a structured observation of the video using the sample observation schedule on Activity Sheet 6.1. They should tick in the box whenever the relevant event happens in the video.

    The adult facilitator may need to pause the video occasionally in order to give the children time to tick their observation schedule. This is why video-recording an observation is useful, as researchers can stop and start and go back to bits they missed.

2. Compare the observation schedules completed by the children and discuss what they think about carrying out a structured observation.

3. Ask the children what they should do after designing a structured observation schedule. They need to 'pilot' it before actually using it.

Practising the observation schedule to get used to it before using it will also be a good idea.

Real-time observation or suspended-time observation

1. Explain to the children two ways of recording observation, 'real-time' and 'suspended-time' observation, based on Box 6.4.

Box 6.4 Real-time and suspended-time observation

In 'real-time' observation, researchers record what they observe at the very moment it takes place.

In 'suspended-time' observation, researchers video-record the events and then, while watching the video footage later on, they note down what they observe.

---

2. Discuss with the children an advantage and a disadvantage that video-recorded observation might have in comparison to real-time observation.

An advantage of video-recording observation is, as in the previous activity, that recorded observation can be revisited as many times as necessary. A disadvantage is that a video camera can only capture a limited field of vision and may miss things that happen outside its frame. So it will be helpful to take notes too whilst video-recording observation.

Ethical issues associated with conducting observation

Discuss with the children what ethical issues they might need to think about when using observation, based on Box 6.5.

Box 6.5 Ethical issues to consider when conducting observation

- People need to be informed before they are observed: 'informed consent'.
- Data and findings from observation must be kept 'anonymous' and 'confidential'.
- Video data must be stored securely and deleted after the research has been completed.

For ethical reasons, original data collected from research participants are usually destroyed after the research. However, the adult facilitator needs to explain to the children that they must not destroy data before they are absolutely certain that they have finished analysing them. Once data are destroyed, even if the children need to check something in it later on, it will be impossible to do so.

Comparing observation with interviews and questionnaires

1. Ask the children what advantages observation might have compared with interviews and questionnaires (this was addressed briefly at the beginning of the session).

   When asked questions during interviews or in questionnaires, people might not give an accurate or honest answer about how they behave in a certain situation. In some cases, the research participants may not even know how they will behave in the situations they are being asked about. Using observation allows the researcher to see how they actually behave in these situations.

2. Discuss with the children the challenges of using observation compared with interviews and questionnaires, based on Box 6.6.

Box 6.6 Some challenges to consider when conducting observation

- Some people might behave differently from the way they usually behave if they know that they are being observed. This problem may decrease if the researcher carries out many observations of them, as they may eventually become used to the research situation and behave as they usually do.

- Some people might not like being observed and refuse to take part in the research.

- The researcher may not be able to observe everything that is going on. This problem may decrease if there is more than one researcher conducting the observation.

Using visual materials as data

1. Ask the children how they might be able to use 'visual materials' such as photographs, drawings or maps in collecting data from research participants.

   Depending on the research topic, drawings or photographs taken by research participants may help a researcher to better understand what they think or feel than what they simply say (when interviewed) or write down (on a questionnaire).

2. Distribute copies of Activity Sheet 6.2. The children think about how Jenny in the activity sheet might use photographs, drawings or maps to help collect data from her research participants.

   In a plenary, the children present how they might use photographs, drawings or maps in Jenny's research. Lead the discussion based on Box 6.7 and Box 6.8.

Box 6.7 Using photographs in Jenny's research (Activity Sheet 6.2)

Jenny could ask her research participants to take pictures of the points in the roads that they think are 'safe' or 'not safe' and write an explanation for this for each photo.

If the research participants are not good at writing or if Jenny prefers to hear from them directly so she can ask probing questions, she could ask them to explain their photos in person.

In this case, the photos taken by her research participants and their explanations will be Jenny's data. By looking at the photos, Jenny may be able to understand more clearly what her research participants think is 'safe' or 'not safe' for them.

Box 6.8 Using drawings or maps in Jenny's research (Activity Sheet 6.2)

Asking child research participants to take photographs may not always be possible because not all of them may have access to a camera or know how to use one. In this case they could be asked to draw.

Jenny could ask her research participants to draw a map of their journey from home to school and mark on it any points where they think it is not safe to walk or travel. Jenny could then ask her research participants to explain why they marked those points on their map as 'not safe'. This will help Jenny to understand more clearly where they are and why her research participants think those places are not safe.

3. Discuss with the children whether any of them think using visual materials might be useful for their own research and, if so, how they think they may use them.

Using visual materials when doing interviews or using a questionnaire

1. Explain that the children could use photographs or drawings with the other data collection methods that they have looked at before. Ask them to think about how they might do this.

A researcher can use photographs or drawings in their interviews or on a questionnaire to help the research participants understand what a question is about (see an example in Box 6.9). Showing a relevant photo or drawing can help the research participants to express what they think or feel more easily.

Box 6.9 Using visual materials in interviews: an example

A child researcher is interested in finding out what the children in his school think about the facilities in the school playground. He made an interview schedule with a list of questions to ask and also took photos of different facilities in the playground to show to his interviewees when asking questions relevant to each of them. Showing photographs to his interviewees (or inserting photos on his questionnaire) was helpful because not all the children understood what the researcher meant by the names of the facilities alone.

2. Ask whether any of the children think using some visual materials in their interviews or questionnaire might be useful.

Using visual materials when reporting the research findings

 The last session of this book focuses on how to report research findings. Before this session, the children can be given some preliminary tips on reporting their findings, as follows.

Explain to the children that when writing a report or making any other presentation materials about their research, they can insert visual materials if these materials help to illustrate their findings more clearly to the readers or their audience.

When reporting their research findings, the children will need to explain how they found them out (i.e. the research process, including how they collected their data and how they analysed them) so that their readers will be able to assess the findings for themselves. Inserting some photos or drawings to illustrate the research process, as in the example in Box 6.10, may make the presentation of the research findings more informative and/ or interesting.

Box 6.10 Using photos or drawings when reporting research: an example

A child researcher was interested in the interactions between her teacher and her classmates during maths lessons. She interviewed both her teacher and classmates about their interactions. She also carried out observation of several maths lessons, using a structured observation schedule.

To illustrate the classroom setting of her observation, she drew a map of her classroom to mark where her teacher usually stood and moved during the lessons, the seating arrangements of her classmates and where she sat while observing the lessons. She included this drawing in her research report to show readers the setting where her observation of the maths lessons took place, and to help them consider for themselves what benefits and limitations her observation might have had.

Ethical issues associated with using visual materials

Ask the children what ethical issues they might have to think about when using visual materials. Lead the discussion based on Box 6.11.

Box 6.11 Ethical issues when using visual materials

- When using a photo, the researcher must get 'consent' from all the people in the photo.

- If the researcher uses photos in their research report or presentation materials, they need to think about how they will ensure the 'anonymity' of the people in the photos. Without their permission, the people's names should not be put with the photos. If the people prefer, their faces could be blurred.

- When using photos, drawings or anything else that the research participants produced in a research report or other presentation materials, the researcher must acknowledge them accordingly.

The advantages and disadvantages of using visual materials

Distribute copies of Information Sheet 6.2 and go through the advantages and disadvantages of using visual materials with the children.

Consent forms for collecting data

1. Distribute copies of two sample 'consent forms'.

    The first form is to be signed by the research participants when the researcher is interviewing and taking photos of research participants who are under 16 years old. The second form is to be signed by the research participants' parents or guardians when the researcher is interviewing and taking photos of research participants who are under 16 years old. When the research participants are 16 years old or older, consent forms need to be signed only by them.

    The children can make their own consent forms by modifying the sample consent forms appropriately, based on what their research is about, their data collection method(s) and whether their research participants are younger than 16.

2. Referring to Box 6.12, explain to the children when they need to get consent forms signed by their research participants.

Box 6.12 When does a researcher use consent forms?

If the researcher uses a questionnaire to collect data and the questionnaire does not ask the research participants to write down any information by which they could be identified (anonymous questionnaire), the consent forms do not need to be signed by the participants in advance of data collection. If an anonymous questionnaire is used without requiring the research participants to sign a separate consent form, the questionnaire needs to have, at the beginning, a statement such as 'by completing this questionnaire, you are indicating your consent to take part in this research'. However, if there is any chance that the identity of the research participants completing the anonymous questionnaire will be known to the researcher, a separate consent form needs to be signed by the participants.

As for most of the other data collection methods, including interviews and observations, the consent forms need to be signed by the research participants in advance.

If the research participants are under the age of consent (for example, this is 16 years old in the UK) and if the researcher wants to interview, observe, video-record or take photos of them as part of their data collection, they need to get the consent forms signed also by the research participants' parents (or guardians).

Wrap up

1. Ask the children to think about which data collection method might be the most helpful to investigate their own research topic or question.

2. Explain to the children that in the next session they will decide from whom they will collect the data for their research, before making data collection tools and starting to collect data.

A sample observation schedule (for observing a class)

Date and time of observation:

Place of observation:

Any other information that will be useful to note:

What happened	Unit of observation					
	0 to 5 minutes	5 to 10 minutes	10 to 15 minutes	15 to 20 minutes	20 to 25 minutes	25 to 30 minutes
1 The teacher explains something to the whole class						
2 The teacher asks a question to the whole class						
3 The teacher asks a question to a particular pupil						
4 A pupil answers the teacher's question						
5 Several pupils answer the teacher's question						
6 The teacher acknowledges a pupil's answer						
7 The teacher acknowledges several pupils' answers						
8 Other (examples …)						

© 2017 Chae-Young Kim, Kieron Sheehy and Lucinda Kerawalla, *Developing Children as Researchers*, Routledge

Using visual materials when collecting data

Jenny, a child researcher, is interested in finding out what her classmates think about the safety of the roads that they walk or travel on by any other means when coming to school. In order to investigate her research topic, she could ask her classmates various questions in an interview or give them a questionnaire to fill in.

Might it be more helpful if, instead, Jenny uses photographs, drawings or maps in collecting data from her research participants? If so, how could she use them?

Comparing structured observation and unstructured observation

Structured observation	Unstructured observation
Researchers decide in advance what to look for during the observation. The list of these things should be those most relevant to their research topic or question.	Researchers do not decide in advance the specific things they will look for in their observation.
Researchers make an 'observation schedule' that lists the specific things that they will look for.	Researchers record anything that they notice and think is 'important' in relation to their research topic or question.
Researchers carry out the observation, marking systematically on the observation schedule whenever the things that they are looking for occur.	Although the researchers do not use a detailed observation schedule like that used in structured observation, they take notes of what they observe and those notes become their data.

Advantages and disadvantages of using visual materials

Advantages	Disadvantages
Using visual materials can help the research participants, including those who cannot read and/or write, to take part in the research more actively than simply giving answers during an interview or by being watched during observation.	The researcher must get consent from all the people in a photo and some people may not like being photographed.
Visual materials can help stimulate the discussion between the researcher and their research participants.	When using photos taken by the research participants as part of data collection, arranging for the research participants to take photos might not always be easy or possible.
	For example, not all the research participants may have a camera; some participants may not know how to use a camera; or some of them may not like taking photos, so they may refuse to take any.
Visual materials can help researchers make their points more clearly when reporting their findings and in explaining how they found them.	Researchers might assume that children like drawing, but some children may not like drawing.

This is a sample consent form for interviewing and taking photos of research participants who are younger than 16 years old. A child researcher may modify this sample consent form to fit her or his data collection needs. The child researcher may also modify this consent form to make one for research participants who are 16 years old or older.

Consent form (1)

My name is: ....

I am carrying out research to find out about: ....

About the interview

I would like to interview you about your thoughts on my research topic. Before doing so, I need your permission. During the interview, if you do not want to answer a question, you may just say 'pass'. You may also change your mind and you are free to leave the interview at any time.

With your permission, I will audio-record what you say to me. If you do not like being audio-recorded, I will take notes of your answers. Anything you say to me will be treated as confidential. This means I will not tell anyone it was you who said this and that. I may use quotes from you (parts of what you say) in my research report or any other presentation materials. If so, you will remain anonymous and this means I will not disclose any information by which you can be identified.

I will store any data that I obtain from you securely and will not give it to anyone else. I will not put any recordings of what you say to me on the Internet. I will destroy them once my research is finished.

About photos

For my research I would also like to take some photos of you when you are .... However, you are free to ask me to stop photographing you at any time.

I might use photographs of you in my research report or any other presentation materials. In this case, I will not include your name. I might put my research report or any other presentation materials, with photographs of you, on the Internet to show other people what I have done in my research. I might share my report or any other presentation materials with other people. In these cases, would you like your face pixelated or blurred?

(Please tick one)   Yes ☐   No ☐

I will store all photographs of you securely and will not give them to anyone else. I will destroy them once my research is finished.

I will also get permission from your parent or guardian for your participation in this research. I will only interview and take photos of you if I have permission from both you and your parent or guardian.

If you agree to the above, please sign here: ....

Write your name in capital letters here: ....

Write the date here: ....

This is a sample adult consent form to get a parent's or guardian's permission to interview and take photos of her or his child who is younger than 16 years old. A child researcher may modify this sample consent form to fit her or his data collection needs.

Consent form (2)

My name is: ……………………………………

I am carrying out research to find out about: ……………………………………………

About the interview

I would like to interview your child about her/his thoughts on my research topic. Before doing so, I need your permission. During the interview, if she/he does not want to answer a question, she/he may just say 'pass'. She/he may also change her/his mind and is free to leave the interview at any time.

With your permission, I will audio-record what she/he says to me. If she/he does not like being audio-recorded, I will take notes of her/his answers. Anything she/he says to me will be treated as confidential. This means I will not tell anyone it was she/he who said this and that. I may use quotes from her/him (parts of what she/he says) in my research report or any other presentation materials. If so, she/he will remain anonymous and this means I will not disclose any information by which she/he can be identified.

I will store any data that I obtain from her/him securely and will not give it to anyone else. I will not put any recordings of what she/he says to me on the Internet. I will destroy them once my research is finished.

About photos

I would like to photograph your child doing ....
Before doing so, I need your permission. However, you may change your mind and are free to ask me to stop photographing your child at any time.

I might use photographs of your child in my research report or any other presentation materials. In this case I will not include her/his name. I might put my research report or any other presentation materials, with photographs of your child, on the Internet to show other people what I have done in my research. I might share my report or any other presentation materials with other people. In these cases, would you like your child's face pixelated or blurred?

(Please tick one)   Yes ☐   No ☐

I will store all photographs of your child securely and will not give them to anyone else. I will destroy them once my research is finished.

I will also get permission from your child about her/his participation in this research. I will only interview and take photos of your child if I have permission from both you and your child.

If you agree to the above, please sign here: ....

Write your name in capital letters here: ....

Write your child's name in capital letters here: ....

Write the date here: ....

Choosing research participants and drawing up a research plan

Session objectives

- Start to draw up a research plan
- Understand the key issues associated with choosing research participants
- Know some sampling methods that are frequently used in social research
- Understand what 'generalising' research findings means and why a researcher needs to be careful about doing so

Key vocabulary

Target population, sample, sampling, random sampling, stratified random sampling, convenience sampling, snowball sampling, representative, generalise

Resources

- Copies of Activity Sheets 7.1 and 7.2, Information Sheet 7.1, and Sampling Illustrations 7.1 to 7.5
- Two sets of small paper cards: one set with the numbers B1 to B180 on them and another set with the numbers G1 to G180 on them (see the end of this session for these cards; and, when photocopying the cards, it may be helpful to print each set on paper of a different colour and to enlarge their size)
- Two bags (or hats) to put the two sets of paper cards into

Introduction: drawing up a research plan

1. Distribute copies of Activity Sheet 7.1, 'My research plan'. Ask the children to see how many of the questions on the plan they can currently answer. Most children are likely to be able to answer the questions about their research topic and what kinds of data they might like to collect and how.

2. Explain that after this session they will be able to answer more questions in their research plan, and in this session they will learn about how to decide who their research participants will be (i.e. who they will collect data from and/or about).

Target population, sample and sampling

1. Distribute copies of Activity Sheet 7.2. In pairs or small groups, the children discuss the questions on the activity sheet.

   In a plenary, ask who Emma's research participants should be (who should Emma collect her data from?) and then explain the points in Box 7.1.

Box 7.1 Target population

A 'target population' is the entire group of people with which the research topic or question is concerned.

Because Emma's research topic says 'children in my school', this is her target population. Emma could ask all 360 children in the school to take part in her research.

---

2. Ask the children, in the following case, what Emma could do.

   If Emma has the time to collect data from all the children in her target population she may decide to do this. However, what she does will depend on how much time she has for her research and how she decides to collect her data. As in the previous sessions, some data collection methods need a relatively long time to complete. In this case, it might be difficult for Emma to involve all the children from her target population in her research. What else could she do?

3. Explain that Emma may have to choose a smaller number of children out of her target population and then, based on Box 7.2, explain what 'sample' and 'sampling' mean.

    The children will learn about the four methods of sampling that are frequently used in social research. Suggest that, while doing so, they think about which one might be best for their own research.

Box 7.2 Sample and sampling

A smaller group selected out of a target population is called a 'sample' and the process of choosing this smaller group is called 'sampling'.

There are many different ways of sampling and some of the most frequently used ones are 'random sampling', 'stratified random sampling', 'convenience sampling' and 'snowball sampling'.

 ## How many research participants are sufficient for a sample?

If the researcher is interested in finding some general patterns in their target population, the bigger the sample size is, the better it is. This is because it is more likely that a bigger sample will better represent the overall characteristics of the target population than a smaller one.

It is often difficult to know what an appropriate sample size is. Identifying a 'saturation point' is one way of doing so. This is the point when a researcher feels that she or he has reached a sufficient understanding about the research topic and does not think she or he is getting any additional understanding about it from the additional number of research participants.

There are also some statistical measures to use in estimating a sufficient sample size. However, these measures, which are related to the concept of statistical power or significance (indicating the level of possibility that the findings are not merely a result of chance), are probably too complex to deal with regarding children's research projects.

Random sampling

1. Using Activity Sheet 7.2, explain that Emma could first decide how many children she can manage to investigate in her research and

then choose the required number of children from her target population 'at random'.

Box 7.3 Random sampling

In 'random sampling', each person in the target population, in principle, has the same chance of being chosen as anyone else.

2. Demonstrate how to do random sampling using the two sets of numbered cards (at the end of this session) in the following way: Assume that Emma has decided to choose 60 children as a sample from her target population of 360 children. One way of random sampling would be for Emma to put all the names of her target population in a bag and then pick 60 out of them without looking.

    To illustrate random sampling, assume the cards numbered G1 to G180 represent all the girls' names in Emma's target population and B1 to B180 represent all the boys' names. Put all of the cards in a bag and then ask a child, or a couple of them, to pick 60 of the paper cards out of the bag without looking into the bag. Each name in the bag has the same chance of being picked as any other because the children do not know who will be picked out. In other words, the numbers picked out of the bag are chosen 'randomly'.

3. Show the children Sampling Illustration 7.2 on 'random sampling' to help consolidate their understanding.

Stratified random sampling

1. Using Activity Sheet 7.2, ask the children how Emma should select her sample if she wants to find out if there are any differences between the boys and girls at her school.

    Let the children see whether the cards they selected in the previous random sampling activity divided equally or similarly between 30 girls' cards and 30 boys' cards. It is very unlikely that this was the case: there will probably be an unequal number of boys and girls.

    In order to ensure that she has a similar number of boys and girls in her sample to make a fair comparison between them, Emma could decide to choose 30 girls randomly from all the girls in her target population and 30 boys randomly from all the boys in her target population.

Box 7.4 Stratified random sampling

Dividing the target population into smaller groups and then choosing samples randomly from each one is called 'stratified random sampling'.

2. To demonstrate how they can do stratified random sampling, ask the children to sort the paper cards into boys' cards and girls' cards. Put the boys' cards into one bag and the girls' cards into another. Then, ask a child to pick out 30 cards from the bag with boys' cards and ask another child to pick out 30 cards from the bag with girls' cards.

3. Ask what Emma (on Activity Sheet 7.2) should do if she is interested in finding out whether and how her findings might differ between each year group.

   They can pick out a certain number of children randomly from each year group. Furthermore, if they want to compare the findings between boys and girls from each year group, they could also pick at random a number of boys and girls respectively from the boys and girls in each year group.

4. Show the children Sampling Illustration 7.3 on 'stratified random sampling' to help consolidate their understanding.

Convenience sampling

Ask the children what 'convenience sampling' might be before explaining it based on Box 7.5. Then show them Sampling Illustration 7.4 on 'convenience sampling' to help consolidate their understanding.

Box 7.5 Convenience sampling

When random sampling is difficult to do and the researcher cannot approach suitable research participants easily, she or he may decide to choose people who can be approached relatively easily. The sampling was conducted 'conveniently'.

Snowball sampling

1. Ask the children what 'snowball sampling' might be before explaining it based on Box 7.6. Show the children Sampling Illustration 7.5 on 'snowball sampling' to help consolidate their understanding.

Box 7.6 Snowball sampling

The researcher may ask existing research participants whether they know other people in the target population who could also be research participants. If the researcher then asks these new research participants the same thing, the size of the sample will grow gradually like a rolling snowball.

2. Ask the children who is the target population of Chris's research (on Activity Sheet 7.2), and how he could gather his sample of research participants.

   Chris's target population are all the children in his school who have more than one younger brother or sister. However, he does not know many children who have more than one younger brother or sister at the moment. He could ask his research participants whether they know other children who have more than one younger brother or sister.

Representativeness and generalisation

1. Using the examples of Emma's and Chris's research on Activity Sheet 7.2, ask the children (if they investigated their research topics using a sample), whether they can say that what they found is also true of all the people in their target population. In other words, can they 'generalise' what they have found from their sample to their target population as a whole?

   The answer to this question will depend on whether their sample is 'representative' of the target population. Explain to the children, based on Box 7.7, what 'representative' and 'generalise' mean.

Box 7.7 'Representative' and 'generalise'

'Representative' is when the sample has the same characteristics as the target population from which it was selected in a range of aspects that may influence the research findings (for example, age, gender, ethnicity, disability (types, length of time having disability, etc.), where they live, family composition, their own level of education, level of parental education, family income, daily diet and so on).

To 'generalise' is to assume that what was found by using the sample, which is a small group of the target population, applies to the target population as a whole. So, when a sample is 'representative' of the target population, the researcher can 'generalise' the findings from the sample to the whole target population.

2. Ask the children whether a sample selected using random sampling, stratified random sampling, convenience sampling and snowball sampling can be 'representative' of their target population. In other words, can they 'generalise' the findings from each type of sample to the target population?

   The points in Box 7.8 can be explained to the children.

Box 7.8 Representativeness and sampling

- Samples selected by random sampling tend to be more representative than those formed by using convenience sampling and snowball sampling. However, this does not apply when the sample size selected through random sampling is small.
- The bigger the size of the sample, the more likely that the sample will be representative of the target population as a whole.
- When the target population is small, any sample will need to be proportionately bigger than when the size of target population is very big, in order to be representative.
- As the children's research will usually have a small target population and use small samples, they will need to be very careful about generalising what they find from their sample to their target population.

- Based on what they find from their sample, the children can only say what their target population might be like. For example:

    Emma in Activity Sheet 7.2 used a sample. In this sample, most of her girl participants said that they did not like their physical education lessons because they only learned games that boys were better at.

    If so, Emma can say, 'the girls whom I investigated tended to say that they did not like their physical education lessons because they only learned games that boys were better at'. However, she must NOT say that all the girls whom she investigated or all the girls in her school said this.

3. Distribute copies of Information Sheet 7.1 and the sampling illustrations to the children for their reference purposes.

Drawing up my research plan

Ask the children to take out Activity Sheet 7.1, 'My research plan'. They should now be able to answer the four questions about their research participants on the activity sheet. The children should try and answer these questions.

If they want, the children may try to fill in the question on how they will analyse their data. This can be revisited after the subsequent two sessions on data analysis.

 ### Suggestions for the next steps in the children's research process

1. After Session 7, the adult facilitator may wish to check the children's research plans individually.
2. When most of the children have made decisions about who their research participants will be and how they will collect their data, it may be useful to hold a session where the children present their research plans and give feedback to one another.
3. In Session 3, when discussing 'be ethical', it was explained to the children that they will take the role of an ethics committee for one another's research plans. The adult facilitator can explain to them that

when giving feedback on each other's research plans, they should also consider, as the members of an ethics committee would, whether it is unethical in any way and how any such issues could be resolved.

4. Once they have made a final decision on who they will collect data from, what kinds of data it will be and how they will collect the data, the children can start to make their research tools such as a questionnaire, an interview schedule, an observation schedule or anything else that is appropriate for their research, and then collect data.

5. It will be helpful if the adult facilitator talks about and agrees on the dates by which the children are expected to finish the production of their data collection tools and collecting their data.

6. The adult facilitator may wish to check the children's research tools before they are implemented. It may also be useful for the children to discuss, and give feedback on, one another's research tools. They can certainly pilot their research tools with the other children if their research participants will be children of similar ages.

7. The adult facilitator can make a decision on whether she or he will run the subsequent two sessions on analysing data before or after the children have completed their data collection. Whereas having an understanding about how to analyse data can help the children in designing their data collection tools, if the analysis sessions are conducted after data collection, they may be able to connect the sessions' content more directly to their own data.

8. Concerning the decisions on how to share their research findings on 'My research plan', it may be useful to start discussing with the children with whom, how and where they will share their research findings.

My research plan

What is my research topic or question?

Decisions about my research participants	
Who are my target population?	
Will I investigate the whole target population or use a sample?	
If I will choose a sample, what type of sampling will I use and why?	
If I will choose a sample, who and how many from the target population will be in my sample?	

Decisions about data collection and data analysis	
What information (data) do I need to collect from and/or about my research participants in order to investigate my research topic or question fully?	
How will I collect the data from them?	
How will I analyse the data?	

Decisions about sharing research findings	
With whom will I share my research findings?	
How, when and where will I do so?	

Deciding on research participants

Emma and Chris attend the same school. In their school, there are two classes in each year. Each class has about 30 children and about half of them are girls. In total, there are 360 children in the school.

Emma's research topic is the opinions of children in her school about their physical education lessons.

- Who should Emma collect her data from?
- How many children should she collect data from?

Chris's research question is 'how do children who have more than one younger brother or sister feel about this in relation to their home and school lives?' Chris knows only two children in his own class who have more than one younger brother or sister.

- Who should Chris collect his data from?
- How many children should he collect data from?

Methods of sampling

Random sampling

The researcher chooses her or his research participants from the target population, using a selection method in which each person in the target population has the same chance of being chosen. Random sampling could be carried out as follows, for example:

- Put all the names of the people in the target population into a hat and pick names out of the hat to decide who to include in the sample.
- Assign numbers to all the people in the target population (or the people may already have numbers assigned to them), and pick numbers out of a bag to include in the sample.

Stratified random sampling

In order to ensure the researcher has in the sample at least a certain number of people from different sub-groups within their target population, she or he decides the number of people to choose from each sub-group and then, within each of the sub-groups, chooses the assigned number of research participants randomly. This is used especially when a researcher is interested in investigating the differences and similarities between findings from each sub-group.

An example of stratified random sampling

There are 312 boys and 152 girls in a target population (almost twice as many boys as girls). In order to represent the views of this population accurately, it would be ideal if the sample included twice as many boys as girls.

If the researcher chooses her or his research participants by random sampling from the whole group as described above, there is a chance that she or he may end up choosing as many girls as boys, or far fewer girls than boys (less than half the number of the boys).

If the researcher decides to have 60 participants in her or his sample from the target population, she or he should decide to choose at random 40 from the boys and 20 from the girls. If they do this, the proportion of boys to girls in the sample will be similar to that in the target population.

Convenience sampling

The researcher chooses who to include in her or his sample, based on who is easier to approach among the people in the target population.

Snowball sampling

When the researchers do not know where to find and/or how to approach their research participants, they may start with a small number of research participants whom they already know. They can then ask these participants whether they know any other people who can participate too. In this way, they can continue to find research participants until they feel they have found a sufficient number of people, making their sample size bigger over time like a snowball rolling down a hill.

For example, a researcher wants to undertake research about children who play Scrabble as a hobby, but she or he knows only two children who do so. She or he asks those two children whether they know any other children who play Scrabble too, and using their answers, the researcher may be able to find other children who also play Scrabble.

Target population and sample

Research question: what do children in my school think about their relationships with their classmates?

"In my school there are 625 children. All these children are my target population."

"It is too many for me to investigate. I don't have the time … I will choose a smaller group from these."

"I will choose 60 children from my target population as a sample for my research."

© 2017 Chae-Young Kim, Kieron Sheehy and Lucinda Kerawalla, *Developing Children as Researchers*, Routledge

Random sampling

Research question: how do children in our school cope with their worries?

"Our target population is all of the 625 children in our school."

"We will choose a sample of 60 children from them. How will we do this?"

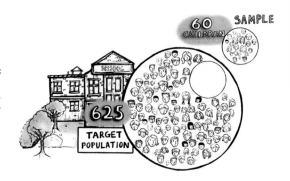

This is the 60th card

"We will put the names of all the children from our school in a hat. Then we will pick out 60 of them 'randomly'."

Stratified random sampling

Research question: how do children in our school cope with their worries?

"Our target population is all of the 625 children in our school."

"We will choose a sample of 60 children from them. Because we are interested in how girls and boys think differently, we will have 30 girls and 30 boys in our sample for comparison."

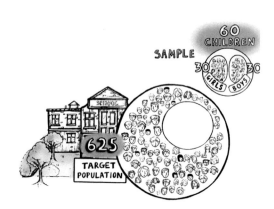

"We will put the names of all the girls in a hat and pick out 30 girls' names randomly."

"We will then put the names of all the boys in the other hat and pick out 30 boys' names randomly."

Convenience sampling

Research topic: the opinions of children with food allergies about our school dinners.

"My target population is all the children in my school
who have food allergies and who eat school dinners."

"I don't know all such children in my school
and also whether they will want to take part in my research ..."

"However, I know at least some of them
and I will investigate them as my sample.
This is 'convenient'!"

Snowball sampling

Research topic: the opinions of children with food allergies about our school dinners.

"My target population is all the children in my school who have food allergies and who eat school dinners. I know only one such child ..."

"This child knows two other children who have food allergies. I can have them as my research participants too!"

"These other children also know some more children who have food allergies. I can also include them in my sample as well.
My sample is becoming bigger like a snowball!"

Number cards to demonstrate random sampling and stratified random sampling

Boys' cards

B1	B2	B3	B4	B5	B6	B7	B8	B9	B10
B11	B12	B13	B14	B15	B16	B17	B18	B19	B20
B21	B22	B23	B24	B25	B26	B27	B28	B29	B30
B31	B32	B33	B34	B35	B36	B37	B38	B39	B40
B41	B42	B43	B44	B45	B46	B47	B48	B49	B50
B51	B52	B53	B54	B55	B56	B57	B58	B59	B60
B61	B62	B63	B64	B65	B66	B67	B68	B69	B70
B71	B72	B73	B74	B75	B76	B77	B78	B79	B80
B81	B82	B83	B84	B85	B86	B87	B88	B89	B90
B91	B92	B93	B94	B95	B96	B97	B98	B99	B100
B101	B102	B103	B104	B105	B106	B107	B108	B109	B110
B111	B112	B113	B114	B115	B116	B117	B118	B119	B120
B121	B122	B123	B124	B125	B126	B127	B128	B129	B130
B131	B132	B133	B134	B135	B136	B137	B138	B139	B140
B141	B142	B143	B144	B145	B146	B147	B148	B149	B150
B151	B152	B153	B154	B155	B156	B157	B158	B159	B160
B161	B162	B163	B164	B165	B166	B167	B168	B169	B170
B171	B172	B173	B174	B175	B176	B177	B178	B179	B180

Girls' cards

G1	G2	G3	G4	G5	G6	G7	G8	G9	G10
G11	G12	G13	G14	G15	G16	G17	G18	G19	G20
G21	G22	G23	G24	G25	G26	G27	G28	G29	G30
G31	G32	G33	G34	G35	G36	G37	G38	G39	G40
G41	G42	G43	G44	G45	G46	G47	G48	G49	G50
G51	G52	G53	G54	G55	G56	G57	G58	G59	G60
G61	G62	G63	G64	G65	G66	G67	G68	G69	G70
G71	G72	G73	G74	G75	G76	G77	G78	G79	G80
G81	G82	G83	G84	G85	G86	G87	G88	G89	G90
G91	G92	G93	G94	G95	G96	G97	G98	G99	G100
G101	G102	G103	G104	G105	G106	G107	G108	G109	G110
G111	G112	G113	G114	G115	G116	G117	G118	G119	G120
G121	G122	G123	G124	G125	G126	G127	G128	G129	G130
G131	G132	G133	G134	G135	G136	G137	G138	G139	G140
G141	G142	G143	G144	G145	G146	G147	G148	G149	G150
G151	G152	G153	G154	G155	G156	G157	G158	G159	G160
G161	G162	G163	G164	G165	G166	G167	G168	G169	G170
G171	G172	G173	G174	G175	G176	G177	G178	G179	G180

Analysing data by counting up

Session objectives

- Understand that data can be examined in, broadly, two different ways: counting up and noticing meanings in them
- Be able to organise data into different groups which need different approaches to analyse them
- Know how to analyse data by counting up

Key vocabulary

Analysing quantitatively, analysing qualitatively

Resources

- Copies of Activity Sheets 8.1, 8.2 and 8.3

Introduction

1. Ask the children whether they have thought about how they will analyse their data and what analysing data might involve.

   'Analysing' data is examining data closely to see whether they contain evidence based on which the researcher can say something significant about the research topic or question.

2. Ask the children whether they remember the three key principles in conducting social research: 'be sceptical', 'be systematic' and 'be

ethical'. All three principles need to be followed closely when analysing their data too.

Discuss with the children, based on Box 8.1, why they need to follow each principle in analysing data.

Box 8.1 Principles for analysing data

Why be sceptical when analysing data?

When looking at their data, researchers need to keep asking themselves whether what looks like 'evidence' is really such evidence. It may appear to support what they think about their research topic or question but how certain can they be about it? Researchers also need to be careful that any personal thoughts or biases they might have do not influence how they interpret data.

Why be systematic when analysing data?

When analysing data, researchers need to have a plan of how they will do it and they will then need to follow this plan in a step-by-step manner so that they do not miss anything significant to their research topic or question.

Why be ethical when analysing data?

When analysing data, researchers need to be careful that no one else, other than the researchers and those who help with their analysis, can access their data. Also they should analyse their data as they are, and not make up anything to make their findings more interesting. This is to respect the research participants and the readers and/or audience of the research.

Handling and sorting data: when to count up and when to consider meaning

1. Ask the children, after collecting their data, how they organised (or will organise) it. Explain what researchers usually do, based on Box 8.2.

Box 8.2 Organising data

a) Organise the data by the types of method used to collect them: for example, questionnaire data, interview data or observation data.
b) Then organise the data by whether they can be immediately 'countable' or not.

2. Explain to the children that data collected by one research method can include both countable data and those that may not be immediately countable, as in the example in Box 8.3.

Box 8.3 A questionnaire generating both countable data and those that may not be immediately countable

Responses to closed questions on a questionnaire are usually immediately countable – because researchers can count how frequently each answer choice was chosen by their research participants – whereas responses to open-ended questions are often not readily countable.

However, sometimes answers to open-ended questions can also be counted up. For example, if the research topic is about school uniform and many research participants wrote the word 'stylish' in their responses to an open-ended question about what they think about it, then the number of participants who wrote 'stylish' can be counted: '16 out of 30 children who answered the question mentioned that our school uniform is stylish.'

3. If this session is carried out after the children's data collection, ask the children to think about whether they have countable data, those that are not immediately countable or both types, and how they might analyse them.
4. Discuss with the children, based on Box 8.4, how they might analyse two different types of data and how they might present evidence from each.

Box 8.4 Analysing data 'quantitatively' and 'qualitatively'

- How to analyse data and then present evidence from them depends on whether they are readily countable or not.

- Countable data are usually analysed 'quantitatively', whereas data that may not be countable are analysed 'qualitatively'.

- Analysing 'quantitatively' means examining data based on the number of times certain answers or points occurred in them. Evidence from quantitative analysis is usually presented in terms of numbers (numbers → quantity → quantitative analysis).

- Analysing 'qualitatively' means looking at words, phrases or sentences and the context in which they occurred in order to see whether they tell the researcher anything significant in relation to their research topic or question (noticing meanings). Evidence from this type of analysis is usually presented in terms of extracts or examples of significant words, phrases or sentences that the research participants actually mentioned (meaning → quality → qualitative analysis).

- Some data are not constituted of any words or sentences that research participants wrote or said, for example, a researcher's notes about how research participants behaved or what happened to them during an observation. In this case, if some behaviours or events look meaningful in terms of their frequency, the researcher can count them up. If it is about a behaviour or event that did not happen frequently but still seems to have some significance, the researcher can examine what meaning it might have in relation to the research topic or question.

5. Explain that in this session they will think closely about how to analyse countable data. In the next session they will learn how to analyse those data that may not be immediately countable.

Counting up data

1. Ask the children what they might have to do first when analysing countable data. For each question that generated such data, they will need to count them up. Using a table may help them to do this in a systematic way.

2. Distribute Activity Sheet 8.1, 'Counting up data using a table'. Explain the activity to the children and give them several minutes to complete it. Where there are children who did not or will not collect any countable data, it will help to pair them with a child who did or will.

   For each question that generated countable data, the children can design a similar table. They can then tick in the cells of the table as they go through each copy of the questionnaire or their interview transcripts. When they have finished with all the copies, they can tally the number of ticks in each cell.

3. When the children have finished the activity, run a plenary session so they can describe to the other children what they did.

Make sense of patterns appearing in the data

1. Ask the children what they might need to do after counting up their data. They need to see whether any patterns appear in them and try to make sense of such patterns.

   Ask the children how they could do this. Encourage them to think about it, looking at the example tally table on Activity Sheet 8.1.

2. Explain the three points in Box 8.5 and then work through the following activities in turn.

Box 8.5 Finding patterns in the data

1. Identify how many and/or what proportion of a group gave a particular answer to each question.

2. Compare the frequency of a particular answer between or across the different groups.

3. Find a trend (a 'trend' is a general direction in which something changes or develops).

---

a) Identifying how many and/or what proportion of a group gave a particular answer.

   Distribute copies of Activity Sheet 8.2. Using the example on the activity sheet, explain how the children can identify how many and/or what proportion of a group gave a particular answer and how these findings can be described, as in Box 8.6.

Box 8.6 Describing proportions

The number, or proportion, of the research participants needs to be stated in the form of 'X out of Y' (for example, eight out of 30 children who responded to this question said they do not like spinach). This clarifies that the number, or proportion, only applies to the number of children who actually answered the question.

b) Comparing different groups: how similar or different are they?
   Consider the question on Activity Sheet 8.2 with the children. For example, 'more girls than boys said that they liked keeping animals in cages' or 'girls were around three times more likely than boys to like keeping animals in cages'.

c) Finding a trend.
   Going back to the example table on Activity Sheet 8.1, ask the children whether they can find any trends in the answers from the boys and girls from Year 4, Year 5 and Year 6. For example, 'more older children tended to choose "agree" and "strongly agree"', or 'more younger children tended to choose "neither agree nor disagree" and "disagree"'.

Be careful when using percentages!

1. Distribute copies of Activity Sheet 8.3. The children should read the example and think about whether using percentages is always useful when reporting their findings, and the reasons why.

2. In a plenary, lead the discussion based on the points in Box 8.7.

Box 8.7 Discussion points for Activity Sheet 8.3

• When the total numbers in the groups being compared are very different (especially when one group is very small), any conclusions from comparing the groups using percentages may not be sound.

• In the example on Activity Sheet 8.3, the number of girls from Year 4 who did not fill in the questionnaire is much larger than that of boys in the same year group who did not do so. So, comparing the outcomes based on only those few girls who responded to the questionnaire may not be fair.

- Whenever a researcher presents percentages, she or he needs to present the actual numbers on which they are based, as in the example on Activity Sheet 8.2. This is to let the readers assess for themselves the soundness of the findings being presented.

In the example on Activity Sheet 8.3, Daniel should say the percentages with their actual numbers, for example: 80%, which was 20 out of 25 boys who answered the question, said they liked their school uniform, whereas 50%, which was three out of six girls who answered the question, said they liked their school uniform.

When reporting findings from counting up data, the researcher needs to let their audience (or readers) know the size of the target population, that of the sample and then the actual number of research participants who took part in their research by filling in questionnaires, agreeing to be interviewed or doing anything else. This is to help the audience to evaluate the findings in relation to the whole picture or context regarding the research topic or question.

Things to think about after analysing countable data

Ask the children, once they have analysed their data, what they might need to think about. Lead the discussion based on the points in Box 8.8.

Box 8.8 Things to think about after analysing countable data

- Researchers need to think about what the outcomes of their analysis tell them about their research topic or question. When they tell others what they found through their research, the specific outcomes of their analysis will be 'evidence' to support these claims.
- When reporting their research, findings from analysing countable data can be presented in tables or various types of graph or chart. Of these different types, researchers choose the format that will illustrate their findings most clearly.

When using a table, graph or chart, the researcher will need to explain what it shows in words too. This provides the audience with the researcher's own interpretation of what the table, graph or chart indicates.

Wrap up

Discuss any questions or comments from the children about how to analyse countable data. Remind them that in the next session they will think about how to analyse data that are not readily countable.

Counting up data using a table

The following table is one that a child researcher drew so that she could tally her data from question five of her questionnaire, a statement: The school council is helpful for improving our school life. She also drew tables like this one for the other questions on her questionnaire. The bars and numbers in each of the cells are the number of children who ticked each answer choice.

Do you think tallying your data in tables like this one will be useful for your research too? On the back of this sheet, please draw a tally table for one or two questions from your questionnaire or interviews. *You do not need to fill in the cells of any tables you draw during this activity.*

Questionnaire/ question 5	Year 4		Year 5		Year 6		Total
Answer choices	Girls	Boys	Girls	Boys	Girls	Boys	
Strongly agree	0	0	| 1	| 1	| 1	|| 2	5
Agree	0	|| 2	||| 3	|||| 4	ⅢⅡ 7	ⅢⅢ 8	24
Neither agree nor disagree	ⅢⅢⅢ 8	ⅢⅢ 7	ⅢⅢⅢ 5	ⅢⅢⅢ 6	| 1	0	27
Disagree	|||| 4	ⅢⅢⅢ 5	ⅢⅢⅢ 5	|| 2	||| 3	| 1	20
Strongly disagree	| 1	0	0	| 1	| 1	| 1	4

Making sense of patterns in data

1. **Identify how many and/or what proportion of a group gave a particular answer**
   In answer to the question 'do you like the idea of keeping animals in cages in the zoo?'

Answer choices	Year 5		Year 6		Total
	Boys	Girls	Boys	Girls	
Yes	5	8	2	10	25
No	9	4	10	2	25
Total	14	12	12	12	50

- *25 out of 50 children* who answered the question, which is 50% of the children, said that they liked keeping animals in cages in the zoo.
- *18 out of 24 girls* who answered the question, which is 75% of the girls, said they liked keeping animals in cages in the zoo.
- *7 out of 26 boys* who answered the question, which is about 26.9% of the boys, said they liked keeping animals in cages in the zoo.

2. **Comparing groups: how similar or different are they?**
   In the example above, are the proportions of boys and girls who said they liked keeping animals in cages similar or different? If they are similar, how similar are they? If they are different, how different are they?

3. **Finding a trend**
   Please look at the table on Activity Sheet 8.1. Can you see any trend among the number of girls and boys from Year 4, Year 5 and Year 6 who chose each answer choice?

Be careful when using percentages!

Please read the following example and consider whether using percentages is always a good way of reporting findings. If so, why is it and if not, why is it not?

Daniel gave copies of his questionnaire on school uniform to all the boys and girls in his school. In Year 4 there are 32 boys and 28 girls in total. From them he collected 25 completed questionnaires from the boys and six from the girls.

He tallied the answers from the questionnaire into tables. To the question of 'do you like our school uniform?', he found that 20 out of the 25 boys in Year 4 who answered the question said 'yes' and three out of the six girls in Year 4 who answered the same question also said 'yes'.

To compare the results between boys and girls in Year 4, Daniel turned them into percentages. So, for the question above, Daniel wrote that 80% of boys liked their school uniform, whereas only 50% of girls liked it.

Analysing data by noticing meanings

Session objectives

- Be able to identify data that need to be analysed by noticing meanings
- Know what 'codes' and 'coding' mean
- Know how to code data
- Know what a 'theme' is and how to identify themes from coded data
- Understand the difference between analysing data by 'counting up' and by 'noticing meanings'

Key vocabulary

Codes, coding, themes

Resources

- Copies of Activity Sheet 9.1, and Information Sheets 9.1 and 9.2
- A few sets of photos or postcards with different landscapes, animals and/ or plants on them

Introduction

1. To review Session 8 on analysing countable data, discuss with the children how they can analyse such data.

2. Ask the children how they could analyse data that do not seem to be countable and how this might be different from analysing countable data. Lead the discussion based on the key points in Box 9.1.

Box 9.1 Reminder from Session 8: analysing 'quantitatively' and analysing 'qualitatively'

- With countable data, the researcher analyses the data 'quantitatively'. This means that the researcher assesses any significance in the data based on the sizes of, and patterns in, the numbers that they get as a result of counting them up.

- When data are not countable, the researcher analyses the data 'qualitatively'. This means that the researcher examines words, phrases or sentences and the context in which they occur, and assesses whether they mean anything significant in relation to the research topic or question.

- When the researcher notices that some words or points occur repeatedly in several research participants' answers to an open-ended question (which she or he had initially classified as data that are not countable), the researcher can also judge how significant they are based on their frequency.

Warm-up activity: sorting things by hidden characteristics

1. Divide the children into small groups. Give each group a set of photos (or postcards) with different landscapes, animals and/or plants on them (the sets of photos do not need to be identical and giving more than ten photos to each group works well). The children think of the different ways in which they could sort the photos.

   The photos can be sorted by various factors, for example: the dominant colour in them, whether they contain trees, whether they show an animal, the season that is shown, whether the photos show the sky, or the particular colour of the sky that is shown, and so on.

2. In a plenary, each group presents how they sorted their photos.
   Then explain to the children that the way in which they sorted their photos is also a way of sorting data that do not seem to be countable, based on the points in Box 9.2.

Box 9.2 The process of sorting data that are not countable

1. Researchers identify an initial set of categories to use to sort their data.

2. They then sort the data systematically using these categories (remind the children that being systematic is one of the three key principles in doing social research).

3. If the categories they chose turn out not to be useful for sorting the data, they should change the categories and sort their data again.
   (In the process of sorting the photos in the activity above, the children may have gone through a similar process of identifying the most suitable characteristics to use to sort them.)

4. They should continue to follow these steps until they think that they have found the most appropriate set of categories to use to sort all of their data.

The children can practise the process above during the following activity.

Coding data

1. Distribute copies of Activity Sheet 9.1. The children, individually or in pairs, read the two sets of observation notes on the activity sheet and think of some categories they could use to sort what is in both sets of observation notes.

   The adult facilitator can give the children some tips on how to start to identify the categories by asking them, for example: 'where are children of different age groups and what are they doing?' and 'where are the adults and what are they doing?'

2. In a plenary, ask the children to present the categories they came up with.

3. Distribute copies of Information Sheet 9.1. Explain that the data in the two sets of observation notes on Activity Sheet 9.1 can be sorted using the categories on Information Sheet 9.1. Then explain the concepts of 'codes' and 'coding' as on the information sheet.

   Explain to the children that different researchers may identify different sets of categories from those suggested on Information

Sheet 9.1, meaning that the suggested categories on the information sheet are not the only answers. This is because different people may identify slightly different meanings in the same data. However, the categories identified by different researchers should not be too different.

4. Using the list of codes on Information Sheet 9.1, the children code the two sets of observation notes in Activity Sheet 9.1. When they have finished their coding, go through the observation notes together, pointing to the places where each code could have been marked.

 Some researchers use computer software programs that help them to code data such as *NVivo* or *Atlas*.

Making sense of coded data

1. Ask the children what they could do next with their coded data. Prompt them to think about whether they could identify a common story emerging across a couple or more codes, or the places where these codes were marked.

    Based on Information Sheet 9.2, lead the discussion on 'themes' and its relationship with 'codes'. Ask the children whether they can think of any other themes using their own coding of the observation notes on Activity Sheet 9.1.

2. Explain that they can apply the way they have analysed observational data in this session to other kinds of data that are not countable, such as those from open-ended questions from interviews or questionnaires. For example, in long answers to an open-ended question from interviews, they can try to find common codes and themes that emerge across answers from different interviewees.

Counting data that were classified as 'not countable'

Ask the children to think if there might be any other ways of analysing data that they classified as 'not countable' (this was discussed briefly in Session 8 and also at the beginning of this session). Then lead the discussion based on Box 9.3.

Box 9.3 Counting data that were classified as 'not countable'

Researchers could count the number of times that a code appears in the data if they think doing this helps them to say something significant about their research topic or question. This is where a way of analysing countable data is combined with analysing data that are not countable.

When reporting findings from this analysis, they can tell how often a certain code or examples associated with it occurred in the data. However, they do not report it using exact numbers as in 'six times in one particular research participant's answer or 32 times across 12 research participants ...' This is because the data were not countable in the first place and, as mentioned above, using the same data, different researchers might have come up with somewhat different sets of codes. So, precise numbers in terms of the frequency of any codes do not have as much meaning as with those with immediately countable data.

When reporting the frequencies in data that are not immediately countable, they could use expressions such as: a certain code or examples associated with it appeared 'many', 'some' or 'a few' times in a research participant's answers, or from 'many', 'some' or 'a few' research participants.

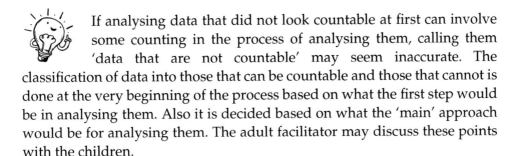 If analysing data that did not look countable at first can involve some counting in the process of analysing them, calling them 'data that are not countable' may seem inaccurate. The classification of data into those that can be countable and those that cannot is done at the very beginning of the process based on what the first step would be in analysing them. Also it is decided based on what the 'main' approach would be for analysing them. The adult facilitator may discuss these points with the children.

Reporting findings from analysing data that are not countable

Discuss with the children how they might report the findings from analysing data that are not readily countable. Lead the discussion based on the points in Box 9.4.

In the discussion, remind the children that when reporting their research, researchers need to tell their readers or audience about the process they used to come up with the findings, so that the readers can evaluate the findings for themselves.

Box 9.4 Reporting findings from data that are not countable

- When reporting findings from data that are not countable, a researcher needs to tell the readers or audience what categories of codes she or he used in analysing them, and the themes that they identified based on these codes.

- If it is possible to tell how often a certain code or theme appeared, the researcher can report the frequency as discussed above.

- If the data are from interviews or a questionnaire, in order to provide the readers or audience of the research with a clearer sense of what the research participants actually said or wrote, the researcher could quote some examples of what they said or wrote under the identified themes.

Wrap up

1. Discuss with the children how they might analyse their own data.

2. Ask the children to take out Activity Sheet 7.1, 'My research plan', and try to fill in the question about how to analyse their data.

 The children will need some individual time to analyse their data. It will be useful to decide with them when their analysis needs to be done by. They may also need some individual support with their analysis.

Analysing observation notes

Ellie was interested in finding out how children and adults make use of the space and equipment in the playground of the local park. In order to investigate this research topic, she carried out observation of the playground every day for two weeks between 4.00 pm and 5.00 pm. While Ellie did not decide specifically what to look for in advance, because she was interested in how children of different age groups and adults used the playground, she focused on observing this and anything else that drew her attention. Ellie used an audio-recorder to record her verbal descriptions of what she was observing and transcribed the recordings later.

The two sets of observation notes shown were selected from 14 sets of observation notes that Ellie made. After reading these two sets of notes, please identify a list of categories that you might use to sort what is in them. Please note that in reality, this list of categories should be created based on all 14 sets of observation notes, but in this activity we practise identifying the categories using only the two sets of notes.

How Ellie addressed ethical issues in her research

Ellie was observing a public space where people come and leave frequently, so it was not feasible for her to get consent in advance from the people whom she observed. Instead, before doing the observations, she contacted the local council office to tell them about her research and what she intended to do. Then, when she carried out her observations, she sat quietly in a corner of the playground, trying not to be intrusive to anyone and not to pose any harm to them. Furthermore, whenever anyone approached her to ask what she was doing, she explained what her research was about. To ensure her own safety, Ellie's elder sister, who is a college student, accompanied her to the park.

Observation notes:
Thursday 5 May, 4.00 pm–5.00 pm, Green Tree Park

As I sit down in a corner of the playground, two women and a man with four small children are leaving the playground.

Three women with buggies in front of them are sitting on one of the benches, talking to each other. Near the women, two toddlers (girls) are playing on the grass.

Four girls who seem to be of early secondary school age (maybe 12 or 13) are sitting in a circle in a corner of the grassed area.

One boy and a girl, both of them probably of pre-school age, are climbing up and down the slide. A man is reading a book on a bench behind the slide.

A boy who may be around 11 or 12 years old is on a swing, laughing loudly and pushing and pulling his legs to go higher. Another boy who looks to be of the same age pushes his friend on the swing. The boy on the swing laughs more loudly. One of the other two swings is broken. The second boy is now hanging on the broken swing, trying to swing on it.

One of the women with buggies stands up from the bench and says good-bye to the other women. She holds the hand of one of the two little girls and then, pushing her buggy, leaves with the girl. The other girl goes to the buggy in front of the woman who seems to be her mum, looks into the buggy and plays with the baby inside.

Three boys who seem to be 12 to 13 years old appear on skateboards, riding them on the paved area next to the grass.

The two boys on the swings leave the playground on their bikes.

Another boy appears on a skateboard and high-fives with the other three boys on skateboards.

The other two women with buggies stand up from the bench and leave, pushing the buggies and taking the little girl with them.

The two small children who were playing on the slide run to the swings. The man on the bench closes his book, follows them and leaves the playground with the children.

Two girls who may be of upper secondary school age (around 15 or 16) come and sit on the bench where the man with a book had been sitting a minute ago.

A young woman and a man come and sit on the bench where the three women with buggies had been sitting.

The four girls who had been sitting in a corner of the grassed area now leave.

Three boys who look to be 15 to 16 years old appear, riding skateboards. The paved area becomes crowded.

The other four boys on skateboards leave the paved area, go onto the grass and start to play football.

Observation notes:
Friday 6 May, 4.00 pm–5.00 pm, Green Tree Park

As I enter the playground, I notice the three women with buggies from yesterday are sitting on the same bench. The two toddlers (girls) are walking around the bench, side by side and holding hands.

Two boys and three girls who all look to be of pre-school age are running around the swings. Three women and a man are standing next to the swings talking to each other. One of the girls now sits on a swing, moving it slowly. One of the women sits on another swing and one of the other two girls sits on the woman's lap, hanging onto her. The woman pushes and pulls her legs to move the swing slowly.

Three boys who may be around 12 or 13 in age are playing football in a corner of the grassed area.

A man and a pre-school-age girl arrive and go to the slide. He puts the girl onto the slide. One of the two little boys who are running around the swings moves to the slide and one of the three girls at the swings follows him.

Two boys and three girls who seem to be 12 to 13 years old come and sit on the paved area. Sitting in a circle, they start to play a game.

The women and the man at the swings round up their children including the two who were on the slide and then leave the playground. Shortly after this, the three women with buggies also leave the playground with the two little girls.

Three girls who may be 14 or 15 in age enter the playground and sit on one of the benches. They look at their mobile phones and talk to each other.

The man and the little girl at the slide leave the playground. The three boys who were playing football also leave the playground.

A woman with a dog walks into the grassed area and sits on the bench behind the slide.

Three boys who look to be 15 to 16 years old (they seem to be the same boys from yesterday) appear with skateboards under their arms. They start to ride them on the edge of the paved area.

The boys and girls who were playing games in the paved area leave the playground.

Codes and coding

When analysing data that are not countable, the categories used to sort them are called 'codes'. The researcher marks each of these codes next to, or in the margin of the paper close to, where it is relevant. This is called 'coding'. In coding, using different coloured pens to mark different codes may be helpful.

A word, phrase or sentence can be marked by more than one code if it appears to be relevant to more than one of the codes. Coding is a first step in examining a mass of data that are not countable in order to draw out their main points.

An example list of codes for the observation notes on Activity Sheet 9.1

Note: In using the following list of codes, mark either 'F' (female) or 'M' (male) to indicate the gender of relevant people and also a number to indicate how many there were. For example, 'early secondary on paved: M2F3' means that two boys and three girls who are probably of early secondary school age were on the paved area.

- Pre-school on equipment
- Child/children and adult(s) leave
- Early secondary on equipment
- Early secondary on grass
- Early secondary on paved
- Early secondary leave
- Upper secondary on bench
- Upper secondary on paved
- Adult(s) on bench
- Adult(s) next to/on equipment

Identifying themes

A common story emerging across a set of codes is called a 'theme'. Based on the coded data on Activity Sheet 9.1, you might draw out some common stories such as those in the box below. A theme can also be identified based on what may not have appeared as a result of coding – in other words, what may be absent. When identifying and interpreting themes, it is also important to consider the contexts where the codes were marked.

Themes that might emerge from using the codes on Information Sheet 9.1

- Mainly pre-school age children and some early secondary school age children use the playground equipment
- Adults tend to spend time either on the bench or next to the playground equipment

(Based on the order of the codes appearing in the observation notes)

- Adults with small children tend to leave early
- Children who seem to be of upper secondary school age tend to appear later than those who seem to be younger
- Younger children seem to leave the paved area when older children appear

(Based on what has not appeared as a result of coding)

- Children who may be of primary school age do not appear to come to the playground between 4.00 pm and 5.00 pm on a weekday

What do the themes above suggest about how children and adults use the space and equipment in the playground?

Reporting and reflecting on social research

Session objectives

- Be able to tell whether a research project has addressed its topic or question adequately
- Be able to reflect on the various decisions made and actions taken during the research process
- Know what to include when reporting on a research project
- Be able to report on a research project in different formats – for example, a research report, a PowerPoint presentation, a poster or a video presentation

Resources

- Copies of Activity Sheet 10.1, and Information Sheets 10.1 and 10.2
- Sticky notes or a whiteboard

Introduction: has my research addressed the research topic adequately?

1. Ask the children whether they have got to know as much about their research topic as they had expected at the beginning of their research process.

    Ask each of them, in turn, to tell what their research topic or question is and then, in a few minutes, to describe what they have found. If there are too many children to do this individually and in a plenary, the children can do the activity in pairs.

2. Explain to the children that it is possible that a researcher does not always have clear findings as a result of their research; however, this does not always mean that the research was unsuccessful.

    Discuss with the children why this may be so, based on the points in Box 10.1.

Box 10.1 Reflecting on research findings and the research process

Not having clear findings may not be because the researcher did anything wrong, but may be because her or his findings just reflect things as they actually are concerning the research topic or question.

Even if the research was not successful (for example, it did not go as planned or the researcher did something wrong), there might still be things that the researcher learned from the experience. Comparing research with a well-organised foreign trip, as they did in Session 1, we could say that even when many things appeared to have gone wrong during a trip, there might still be lessons that they can learn from these which might help them in their next trip. The same thing applies to research.

So it is important to reflect on what went well and what did not go so well after undertaking a research project.

Reflecting on research

1. Distribute copies of Activity Sheet 10.1, 'How did my research go?' The children can do the activity in pairs.

2. In a plenary, ask volunteers to present what they discussed.

Thinking about why we do research

1. Ask the children what the purposes might be of doing research. They may say various things, including: 'to find out something useful', 'to learn research skills', 'to learn to think critically', 'to learn not to think with biases', 'to learn to be ethical' and so on.

2. Listen to what they say and then lead the discussion based on the points in Box 10.2.

Box 10.2 Why do we carry out research?

A researcher may gain various things by doing research. However, the main purpose of research is to produce knowledge. So, reporting their research and discussing it with other people who may be interested in it – sharing their research and knowledge they have produced – is a crucial part of doing research.

Reporting research that did not go very well and has not found any useful findings can also be a meaningful activity. This is because by sharing and discussing what may have gone wrong and what could have been done differently, the researcher or other people can do research on a similar topic better.

Identifying whom to share the children's research with and how to share it

1. Discuss with the children whom they would like to share their research and its findings with and why. In this discussion, ask the following questions as prompts: 'are there any groups of people whom your research may concern directly and/or indirectly?' and 'are there any other people who may find your research interesting?'

2. Then discuss with them how they will report their research to these people. In this discussion, ask them to consider what they need to think about when deciding how to report their research. Some of the things to think about may include:
    *   What might be the most appropriate format of reporting in consideration of the characteristics of the chosen audience or readers?
    *   If it will be face-to-face reporting, where will it be reported, how will this be arranged and how much time will I have to report my research?

3. Explain to the children that some of the most common forms of research reporting are a research report, a PowerPoint presentation and a poster.

 The adult facilitator may find and show the children examples of research reports, PowerPoint presentation slides and research posters that are available on the Internet.

Discuss with the children how each of the three methods of research reporting might be used, based on Box 10.3.

> ## Box 10.3 Ways of reporting and sharing research
>
> - A research report can be published in print or on the Internet so that many people can access and read it. Of the three forms of research reporting, it can include the most detail about the research.
> - A PowerPoint presentation is usually shown at a conference or a meeting.
> - A poster can be displayed in a public place or event so that many people can see it.

 The children may suggest some other more creative ways of sharing their research than the conventional formats as above (for example, making a short film about their research). If so, and wherever possible, it will be interesting to let them explore these other methods.

Thinking about what to include in reporting research

1. Explain to the children that whichever way they report their research, they will need to include some key points about their research so that people who have not heard anything about their research before can understand it as fully as possible.

   Although the amount of detail they can put into a research report, PowerPoint presentation slides or a poster may be different, there are certain things that they need to include in all three. Discuss with the children what these things might be. Write what they suggest on sticky notes or on the whiteboard.

2. Distribute copies of Information Sheet 10.1. Explain that all ways of reporting research should contain as much information as possible about the questions on Information Sheet 10.1. Go through the list of questions with the children.

3. Ask the children why they might need to tell their readers or audience about the entire research process, including how they collected and analysed their data, instead of just telling them their research findings (some of this was discussed earlier in Session 6). Lead the discussion based on Box 10.4.

Box 10.4 Why do researchers report about the entire research process?

It is a researcher's duty to be honest and transparent about how they conducted their research. This is part of being ethical.

Doing so also allows their readers or audience to be able to decide for themselves whether the research was conducted properly and the reported findings are trustworthy. If the reporting is done in a face-to-face setting, it will allow the audience to ask questions to learn more about the research or make some suggestions about how the researcher might do the research differently next time.

 Even if there is something in their research that the children do not want to report, they need to be honest and report it as it is! The example in Box 10.5 may seem a minor issue. However, this example stresses the point that the researcher needs to be transparent about all issues in her or his research process.

Box 10.5 Reporting research as it is: an example

A child researcher intended to audio-record all of her interviews. However, during one of the interviews, the battery of the audio-recorder ran out and she had to take notes instead. When writing about data collection, she said that she had not audio-recorded all of her interviews.

 ## Structuring a research report

The structure of a research report can vary depending on the length of the report and the overall design of the research project. Researchers decide on the sections of the report and their order, considering how effectively and clearly they can explain the research to readers. A research report can consist of sections including:

- Introduction: this explains what the research is about and why it was important to conduct it, and gives a brief overview of the report.

- Background review: children's research reports often do not have this section. This discusses existing research findings or debates around the research topic or question and how the researcher's own research relates to them.

- Data collection: this section describes the research participants (including how they were selected), the type(s) of data and how they were collected. It also explains how any ethical issues were managed.

- Data analysis: this section shows how the data were analysed. This information can also be presented along with the data collection information as one section, under a section called 'Data collection and analysis'.

- Main findings: here the researcher presents the main findings from her or his research and the evidence to support them. The researcher also mentions any limitations concerning the research and the implications of these limitations for their findings.

- Conclusions: the researcher identifies the conclusions and any relevant suggestions from the research.

Each of the above sections can have subsections with appropriate headings.

▌Producing PowerPoint presentation slides and posters

1. Distribute copies of Information Sheet 10.2, 'Some tips on creating PowerPoint presentation slides'. Go through the list with the children.

    The adult facilitator informs the children that there are various computer programs that can help them to make presentation materials, while PowerPoint is the most widely used among them.

2. If the children decide to make research posters, ask them how big the poster will be and what they might put on their poster.

   The most common research poster sizes are A0 (841 x 1189 mm), A1 (594 x 841 mm) and A2 (420 x 594 mm).

   As above, a similar set of things will be presented on a poster as in a research report and PowerPoint presentation slides, but, given the limited space on the poster, they will be described in a more concise form.

■ Planning a research sharing event and/or actions to take based on research findings

1. If the children decide to hold a research sharing event, discuss with them how they will organise it.

2. If the children's research findings suggest that some actions may need to be taken to change a particular practice or measure, discuss with them what they might need to do and how they might go about doing it.

   Reporting research to relevant people is the first step to doing something about the issue concerned.

■ Wrap up

The children start to work on their chosen form of research reporting.

 After Session 10, and when the children have finished preparing their research reporting materials, the adult facilitator helps them to implement their plans to share their research with other people and/or to take further action regarding their findings.

How did my research go?

Let us reflect upon the decisions that you made and the actions that you took during your research process, using the following list of questions. Think about how these decisions and actions influenced your research results. Also consider, if you did your research again, what different decisions and actions you would take and why.

1. Was my research topic easy or difficult to investigate? Might I investigate a different research topic next time?

2. Was my decision on how to select my research participants appropriate?

3. Was my decision on what kind(s) of data to collect from, or about, my research participants appropriate?

4. Was my decision on the method(s) to collect data appropriate?

5. Did I implement the data collection method(s) appropriately?

6. Was the way I analysed my data appropriate?

7. Did I carry out every stage of my research process ethically?

8. Was my approach to my research always systematic?

9. Did I continue to be sceptical throughout my research process when looking at and interpreting data?

10. Anything else?

Things that I need to try to include in my research report, PowerPoint presentation slides or poster

- What is my research topic or question?

- Why was I interested in my research topic or question? Or why was it important to investigate it?

- Whom did I collect data from or about?

- What kinds of data did I collect?

- How did I collect data?

- What ethical issues did I consider in my research?

- How did I analyse data?

- What are the main findings? (If the space allows, I also need to present evidence to support my claims about the main findings.)

- What is the conclusion of my research? What does my research suggest about the research topic or question in terms of what may need to be done?

- What are the limitations of my research? (For example, what could I not do although it would have been useful? Or, if I did the research again, how might I do it differently?)

- Based on the findings, what further research might be interesting?

Some tips on creating PowerPoint presentation slides

- Think about how many slides would be appropriate in the time allowed.
- On the first slide, put the title of my research, my name and the date.
- Put a heading at the top of each slide so that the audience can keep track of what I am talking about (for example, 'introduction', 'my research topic', 'ethics in my research', 'data collection', 'data analysis', 'main findings' and 'conclusions').
- Put only necessary points on each slide (maybe four or five points at most).
- Use a large font size so that people at the back of a room will be able to read it.
- Be careful when using coloured fonts and backgrounds because they may be difficult for people to read.
- When displaying a chart or table, put a brief explanation about what it is about.
- Include pictures or drawings, if they are relevant, to help make the presentation more interesting.
- Thank the audience for their time and ask for any questions or comments.

Suggested reading

During the research sessions, if questions arise which you and the children seem unable to address satisfactorily, the following list of books may be useful reference points where you can start exploring for solutions. These books are mainly for you as the adult facilitator as they may not be accessible to the children.

Many books on social research are available. Some of them cover the entire range of issues relating to the process – including underlying theories, a range of data collection and analysis methods and how to write up the findings – while others focus on specific sets of topics, for example, particular data collection and analysis methods. A general textbook such as the three books listed under 'Books on social research in general' should often be sufficient for dealing with the majority of questions that may arise during the research sessions. In particular, the second book on the list gives a good overview of social research that is conducted in educational settings. While the principles and methods that the book introduces can be applied to research in other settings, it illustrates them with examples directly relevant to educational matters.

If the questions are specifically about certain types of data – for example, data to analyse quantitatively (countable data) or data to analyse qualitatively (data that do not seem to be immediately countable) – the books listed under either 'Books on quantitative data collection and analysis' or 'Books on qualitative data collection and analysis' should also be helpful. Please note that some books focused on qualitative methods treat them as self-sufficient approaches or a matter of research design (overall research plan), rather than as an issue that is mainly concerned with the data collection and analysis stage of a research project.

Books on social research in general

Bryson, A. (2016) *Social Research Methods*, 5th edition. Oxford: Oxford University Press.

Cohen, L., Manion, L. and Morrison, K. (2011) *Research Methods in Education*, 7th edition. Abingdon: Routledge.

Robson, C. and McCartan, K. (2016) *Real World Research*, 4th edition. Chichester: John Wiley & Sons.

Books on quantitative data collection and analysis

Coolican, H. (2014) *Research Methods and Statistics in Psychology*, 6th edition. Hove: Psychology Press.

Foster, L., Diamond, I. and Jefferies, J. (2015) *Beginning Statistics: An Introduction for Social Scientists*. London: Sage.

Gorard, S. (2003) *Quantitative Methods in Social Science*. London: Continuum.

Books on qualitative data collection and analysis

Braun, V. and Clarke, V. (2013) *Successful Qualitative Research: A Practical Guide for Beginners*. London: Sage.

Mason, J. (2002) *Qualitative Researching*, 2nd edition. London: Sage.

Ritchie, J., Lewis, J., Nicholls, C. and Ormston, R. (2013) *Qualitative Research Practice: A Guide for Social Science Students and Researchers*, 2nd edition. London: Sage.

Index